*To Jocelyn, MAY God Blen And [empower] you [life]. 1/28/06*

# PERSONAL EMPOWERMENT

## HOW TO TURBOCHARGE YOUR LIFE BOTH ON AND OFF YOUR JOB

— by —

*Carole Copeland Thomas*

Milormic Press
Woburn, Massachusetts, USA

# Personal Empowerment:
## How to Turbocharge Your Life Both On and Off Your Job

First Edition
Copyright © 2003 - Carole Copeland Thomas.
All Rights Reserved

ISBN: 0974128309 • Library of Congress Control Number: 2003107588

**Publisher's Cataloging-in-Publication Data**
(Prepared by Cassidy Cataloguing Services, Inc.)
Thomas, Carole Copeland.

Personal empowerment : how to turbocharge your life both on and off your job /
Carole Copeland Thomas. — 1st ed. — Woburn, Mass. : Milormic Press, 2003.

p. ; cm.

Includes bibliographical references.

1.†Success. 2.†Success in business. 3.†Self-actualization (Psychology)
4.†Self-efficacy. 5.†Self-realization. I.†Title.

BF637.S8 T56 2003

158.1—dc21                                        0306

**Disclaimer:** While every precaution has been taken in the preparation of this book, the publisher and author assume no responsibility for errors or omissions. Neither is any liability assumed for damages resulting, or alleged to result, directly or indirectly from the use of the information contained herein. If you do not wish to be bound by the above, you may return this book with receipt to the publisher for a full refund of the purchase price.

**Schools and Corporations:** This book is available at quantity discounts with bulk purchases for educational or business use. For more information please contact the publisher at the address below.

**Milormic Press** • (508) 947-5755
400 West Cummings Park • Suite 1725-154 • Woburn, MA  01801

Printed in the United States of America

Book Design and Typesetting by Positronic Design
800.472.3765 • www.PositronicDesign.com
Cover Photo: Sandy Middlebrooks

# Table of Contents

*Dedicated To
My Children
and My Family*

# *Acknowledgements*

Words cannot express the gratitude I have for the countless friends and relatives who supported me in the creation of this book. It was the legacy of my ancestors who made it possible for my existence. I will forever be thankful to my parents, the late Gwendolyn J. Copeland and the late Wilson A. Copeland, who in their own special way nurtured and loved me unconditionally. Attorney Wilson A. Copeland II, is my big brother who's always cheered me on. To his wife, my sister-in-law, Deborah, I thank you for your counsel and for reading and editing my manuscript. To my daughters, Lorna and Michelle, thank you for allowing me to honestly portray our family by profiling your lives and the life of your beloved brother, the late Mickarl Thomas, Jr.

To my niece, Lauren, your artistic talent and grace are what make you so special. Richard Anderson of Detroit, you are just like family to me. To my Bel Air, Maryland relatives, thank you for always believing in me. Aunt Marguerite Copeland, Cousin Laura Copeland, and my other Maryland cousins, I thank you for your love. To my Columbus, Georgia cousins, thank you for your support. And to my extended Gaines Family members, including Clarence Gaines, Theresa Johnson, and others, you've helped me to explore the rich heritage we share together. To my friends in Detroit, Boston and beyond, you are very special to me.

I could not have completed this project without the eagle eyes of my friends who read chapters, critiqued passages, and made excellent suggestions that improved the book. This group includes Sheila Lennon, Dr.Rhonda Waters, Ph.D., Karen Hinds, Frank McCarthy,

Rich Hamilton, and Maurice Wright. A big thank you goes out to Attorney Jacqueline Jones whose eagle eyes gave the final o.k. to my manuscript.

Robin Thompson, my accountability partner, thank you, for the unending support you've given as we both perfect our literary talents.

Thank you, Juanita Jones Abernathy. Your friendship of nearly 30 years has made all the difference to me. I am honored to know you, your family, and your civil rights legacy so interwoven in the fabric of American history.

Appreciation goes out to Allen Todres, Ronald Walker, II, and Denise Gray-Felder for your warm and thoughtful book endorsements. Virginia Nelson, you are indeed my special friend and constant supporter.

Debra Washington Gould and Nancy Lewis, my inspiration and gratitude will always hinge on your first book, *Sisters Together*. You allowed me to express my early thoughts about my Mikey in a chapter in your book. I can't thank you enough for the years of your support.

To Dr. Earl Avery and all of my friends and colleagues at Bentley College of Waltham, Massachusetts, your support and trust in my abilities mean so much to me. I look forward to a second decade of connection to your esteemed institution.

Thank you, Carolyn Sawyer and Martha Fields for the entrepreneurial support you've given me. Janine and Tom Fondon of Unity First.com, I can't thank you enough for your continued support and for the publicity you've given me in your newspaper.

Because of my religious upbringing, I am a grounded faith-based person. My years growing up at St. Paul AME in Detroit followed by

# ACKNOWLEDGEMENTS

Allen Temple AME in Columbus, Georgia, Mt. Zion. AME in Norristown, Pennsylvania, Charles Street AME in Boston, and now Bethel AME in Boston helped to make me who I am today. Thanks to all who have helped keep me connected to my spiritual foundation. A very special thank you goes out to my pastors, Rev. Drs. Ray and Gloria White Hammond, for always praying and ministering to me whenever I need your loving support.

Dr. Mary Grassa O'Neill, Mary Gormley, and the entire faculty and staff of the Milton Public Schools, thank you for your encouragement, your guidance, and your support.

Mildred Allen, you gave me my first corporate contract. My business success is due in part to your early faith in my ability. Thank you for your continued support and friendship through the years.

A very special thank you to all of my clients who support C. Thomas & Associates. I appreciate The TJX Companies, Jobs For The Future, The Patriots' Trail Girl Scout Council and many others. Kerry Hamilton, Karen Coppola, Rubin Williams, Carmon Cunningham, Chris Sears, and Craig Saline, are just samples of the wonderful client-friends who continue to make my business an ongoing concern.

Dr. Bernadine Nash and Patricia Spence, you gave birth to my radio voice. I will forever thank you for opening the doors of radio broadcasting to me.

A sisterly thank you goes out to the members of my sorority, Delta Sigma Theta Inc. You are all book lovers and support me in all of my endeavors. With gratitude I thank the members of the National Black MBA Association. I have enjoyed my 17-year membership because of your support and encouragement. And a special thanks to my friends and colleagues of the National Speakers Association. You've shown me how to take my ideas and concepts and transform them into a manuscript I am proud of.

To Sandy Middlebrooks, my consummate photographer for over 20 years, your front cover photo captures the empowerment within me. Thank you for your photographic eye that brings my pictures to life.

Thank you, Dave Caputo and the staff of Positronic Design, for your creativity and attention to detail as you artfully executed the design and typesetting of my book. Special thanks to King Printing for skillfully producing my finished product.

To all who have helped to make *Personal Empowerment* a reality, I thank you from the bottom of a grateful heart.

*- Carole Copeland Thomas*

# *Introduction*

Little did I realize a few years ago that empowerment would have such a long lasting impact on my life and business. I had spent years building a diversity and leadership business, and enjoyed the fruits of my labor. In the good times and the bad, I've never stopped my need of developing untapped potential while exploring new ways to expand my business services. In that spirit, adding empowerment to my portfolio created an exciting new dimension to my business activities.

My former client and friend, Ainsleigh Foster, called me one summer day and made a telephone introduction of a young woman she wanted me to meet. That conversation launched a new friendship with Patricia Spence, one of the most effective community activists I've ever met. At that time Pat was an account executive at a local urban radio station, WILD-1090 AM. When the topic of radio programming was discussed, my breakfast meeting with Pat expanded into lunch.

Pat mentioned the desire of the station owner, Dr. Bernadine Nash, to broadcast an empowerment segment on her station. I always had an interest in radio, and Pat suggested I submit a proposal outlining how I would approach empowerment. I enthusiastically submitted my proposal to Dr. Nash, and was flabbergasted when it was accepted in record time. A breakfast conversation had landed me on radio in less than a month. My *"Personal Empowerment Tips"* made their debut on that radio station in September 1999. As a result, my relationship with WILD-1090 lasted until January 2003 when program format changes were made after Dr. Nash sold the station to a large radio conglomerate.

# PERSONAL EMPOWERMENT

I am deeply indebted to both Pat Spence and Dr. Bernadine Nash for their commitment to the concept of empowerment. They supported me and made it possible for me to deliver a positive daily message to my listeners for more than three years. The tips lead to a popular one-hour talk show I created, produced, and hosted for two years. *"Focus On Empowerment"* covered a wide variety of topics, and put me in touch with special guests like Steve Forbes and Iyanla Vanzant.

It is from that serendipitous beginning that this book was born. A conversation that led to a radio program ultimately led to the creation of this book.

Empowerment has now become the umbrella concept for everything that I do both personally and professionally. It's broad enough to shape a lifestyle and redirect a business focus. Empowerment gives a person the courage to achieve the impossible or leave a toxic relationship. Empowerment is the energy you need when you know deep down inside you have what it takes to succeed.

This book will take you through the setbacks, joys, and tragedies I've had in my life. It will show you how I've taken my pain and turned it into new possibilities. Personal Empowerment is designed to help you conquer your fears, set your course of action, and turbocharge your life in a positive new direction. It will change the way you think about yourself.

I encourage you to read this book with pen in hand. Highlight the segments that speak to your soul. Make notes on how you will achieve your goals, once you create that personal roadmap that will take you where you need to go. Use this book as your personal guide to your future. Then share its value with your friends, family members, colleagues, classmates, and students.

Empowerment begins when you believe in yourself. I wish you much success as you take on the world, empower your spirit, and connect with all of the people who come in your path.

*- Carole Copeland Thomas*
June 2003

# PERSONAL EMPOWERMENT

## HOW TO TURBOCHARGE YOUR LIFE BOTH ON AND OFF YOUR JOB

— by —

*Carole Copeland Thomas*

Milormic Press
Woburn, Massachusetts, USA

---

# *Empowerment*

is attained by ultimately creating a personal change agent that will push you to reach your full potential at home, on your job, in your community, in your faith, and throughout the world.

---

# CHAPTER ONE

# *Defining Empowerment*

## Welcome To Your World of Personal Empowerment

*Empowerment is the act of officially giving yourself permission to become the very best YOU on the planet. It's a process of transformation, allowing you to grow in new directions that will stimulate your intellectual capacity throughout your lifetime.*

*Empowerment is attained by ultimately creating a personal change agent, that will push you to reach your full potential at home, on your job, in your community, in your faith, and throughout the world that you call your own.*

Is this a massive concept? Yes. But not an impossible one. To look at empowerment another way, here's a comprehensive definition:

"Empowerment is the application of enhanced personal development both on and off the job. Empowerment allows an individual to move to the next level of life by using skill building techniques, employing appropriate resources, spiritual enlightenment, and creating a commitment to a continuous improvement process."

# PERSONAL EMPOWERMENT

Empowerment speaks to the very nature of the human spirit. It provides an energy source that will help you learn from your mistakes while redirecting your path when your circumstances seem impossible. It's the "kick" you need to get up and find that new job. It's the gentle push you need when you're afraid to go back to school to finish that degree. It's the little voice telling you that you will not fail when your reputation is on the line. It's the voice of reason that tells you it's time to open a new window in your personal life when the door you're used to no longer offers a way out of your situation.

Sometimes empowerment means change. When you experience change you're often exposed to the unknown. And change can be very frightening when the unknown is the only path to our future. This book is designed to help you explore those unknown quantities in an effort to help steady your nerves while you dig deep into your soul for the answers inside of you.

As you begin your empowerment journey, here are 20 questions you should ask yourself:

1. Where do you see yourself in five years?

2. What path is ahead of you in the coming years?

3. Are there roadblocks and obstacles getting in the way of your progress?

4. Are you carrying around baggage of your past that clouds the vision of your future?

5. What resources are readily available to help you move to the next level of your life?

6. What's really holding you back from achieving your dreams?

7. Do you have a vision of your future?

8. What plans are you making to secure your future?

9. Who is currently a part of your support system?

10. Who should be a part of support system?

11. What is your real purpose in life?

12. Are you creating a servant or leadership lifestyle for yourself?

13. Who are you mentoring?

14. Who's mentoring you?

15. What tangible opportunities are waiting for you?

16. Is there balance between your work and family life?

17. What lessons from your past can become the foundation of your future?

18. Are you on target in your career?

19. Are you on target in your personal life?

20. Are you creating a legacy that you can leave for others?

Use these 20 questions throughout this book as you explore the many ways that you can either anchor or reposition your life in a positive new direction.

## Uniqueness is the Key

It all starts with you. Just remember that the first step you make in empowering yourself is recognizing the value of your own uniqueness. Go ahead and open the door of your future and taste the possibility of achieving your dreams, your hopes, and your ambitions.

## Empowerment is Finding the Diamond in the Rough

It's the grinding and polishing that makes a diamond sparkle so brilliantly. With the precision of skilled craftsmen who cut it to perfection, a new diamond is born everyday.

What kind of diamond are you? Are the rough cuts and misshapened stories of your life preventing you from reaching your full potential? Are setbacks and disappointments clouding the opportunities that lie before you? Are you giving away your luster in life?

Take back your brilliance by recognizing that every day is a new opportunity to grind and polish your character, your integrity and your reputation. Move from being a diamond in the rough to convincing yourself that you are a sparkling well-shaped dazzling diamond extraordinaire!

Yes, it will take work, but in reality we're all diamonds in the rough. Every day we chip away at our personality flaws, our weaknesses, our bad habits, our doubts and our suspicions. Sometimes it's all of the pain we endure that actually becomes the polish needed to buff the real essence of our being. When we're in trouble, can't pay our bills, or have locked horns with a colleague or a supervisor, it's hard to realize that those very experiences *can* be used to make us stronger.

I emphasize the word "can" because once a negative experience has ended, we're quick to lock it away in our mental garbage heap.

Empowerment expects that we use those experiences as "polish" for our future. The more we acknowledge the mistakes and causalities of our past, the more we can learn new tactics to strengthen our future.

Diamonds come in all different shapes and sizes. Some are round and brilliant. Some are oval. Others are emerald, while the marquise or princess hold their own unique shape. All that baggage you're carrying around in your life will ultimately determine what kind of diamond you will become.

## Character Building

John Wooden said "Reputation is what you are perceived to be. Character is what you are." Your character is a collection of your thoughts, attitudes, values, beliefs and behavior that determines your uniqueness. Continuously improve your character and you will undoubtedly secure your reputation. If you only concentrate on your reputation, you just may compromise your character.

I'm a firm believer that when you live a seamless life, one where your principles and personal integrity are never compromised, your reputation will succeed. That's the level of character building that will empower you to do your best and become the best man, woman or child in your community.

Build your character and your reputation will follow.

## Developing Self-Respect

How can you ever require others to respect you if you don't respect yourself first? Empowerment takes your self-respect to a whole new level.

Empowerment firmly and gently lets you say NO to the demands of others when the time isn't right, the circumstances are not practical or your gut instincts start talking to you. When you bolster your self respect, you take stock of your own value, your uniqueness, and your unlimited potential of personal possibilities by making them work for you. You stop abusing your body with excess drugs, alcohol, unhealthy relationships, food, or negative self-talk. You learn to discipline yourself with better living.

Fortifying your self-respect is a 24/7, round-the-clock job. Try it, you'll like it, because if you won't respect yourself, who else will?

## Celebrate the Temporary

In New England they say, "If you don't like the weather, stick around, because it will change." Our lives are like that, ever changing, always unpredictable. It makes the temporary so special.

Years ago when I moved to New England, a friend gave me a book entitled **Celebrate The Temporary.** Filled with positive examples of changing your personal perspective on life, the title and its content always stuck with me. What I have learned since that time wraps around the steady unpredictability of our lives and the constant reminder of what we do not control.

What we do control is our attitude and the manner in which we'll react to every EVENT of every single MOMENT. That's what temporary stands for. It's a moment in time, just as fleeting as a breezy New England morning.

So **CELEBRATE YOUR TEMPORARY**. Touch it, feel it, learn from it. It you don't like it, stick around. Another chance is waiting for you.

---

# *Establishing a vision*

is only the beginning of your

empowerment process.

You set goals.

Achieve those goals.

You are encouraged to use

your dreams to determine the

landscape of your vision.

---

# CHAPTER TWO

# *Creating Your Vision*

## Create Your Vision by Following Your Dreams

*What is vision?* It's defined as an unusual discernment or foresight. Vision can also be characterized as the power to see what is NOT evident to the average mind. When you embrace empowerment, you're allowed to reach beyond yourself while setting a new direction that requires you to stretch.

How far can you stretch on your job, at home, or in your community? Can you put aside your past troubles and look forward to a brand new horizon of opportunities? Can you see yourself in a leadership role or accumulating wealth? Can you see the doors of protection and prosperity opening wide for your children or grandchildren? Can you see yourself becoming the vehicle of change for those who can learn from your misfortunes?

A personal vision will take you places never before imagined. See it, believe it, and know that your abilities and your vision will help your dreams come true.

## Create Your Own Vision Statement

I belong to a wonderful congregation that sets aside the month of January each year to concentrate on creating a vision for the New Year. During this month our pastor, Dr. Ray Hammond, MD, MA, delivers a series of sermons that articulates the vision each member of Bethel African Methodist Episcopal Church should consider. We are an ethnically diverse congregation, yet our shared values bind us together in a uniform fashion.

I look forward to our annual "Vision Month," and take it upon myself to carry that concept into my personal life. In January 1998 I created my own vision statement that applies to my life today. It states:

*"Carole Copeland Thomas will capture the essence of the human spirit by delivering messages of hope, interconnection, purpose, courage and faith to people throughout the world."*

Each year from this one vision statement, I create a multi-page document of targeted goals that is broken down into financial, marketing, product development, personal, educational, family and spiritual subcategories. Every goal in each subcategory link back to my vision statement.

**Here are some tips on creating a vision statement for yourself:**

1. Use broad, expandable language in your statement.

2. Don't use the present tense. Use verbs that will connect to your future (Rebecca will capture, Douglas will embrace, Michael will unfold, etc.).

3. Mentally stretch when creating your statement. Don't lock yourself into thinking too small.

4. Find a quiet, peaceful location while you're creating your statement.

5. Write your vision on a large poster board and display it in your home or office as a constant reminder of where you are headed in life.

Creating a personal vision statement and its companion goals will take some time to develop. Think about establishing a multi-year system for yourself so that you merely have to update your goals and vision statement instead of re-creating them year after year.

Empowerment begins when you take charge of your life by creating these necessary tools that will keep you centered, balanced, and focused on your path to success.

## Empower Yourself To Dream

Establishing a vision is only the beginning of your empowerment process. You are also given permission to dream. Through your visualization, you create dreams that ultimately turn into tangible goals and objectives.

What is a dream? The dictionary definition states it clearly, "A dream is a train of thoughts or images passing through the mind in sleep." It further describes a dream as, "A visionary idea, anticipation or fancy... or anything having a dreamlike quality."

Our goals, aspirations, achievements, and accomplishments in life so often start off as dreams, images passing through our minds while we are asleep. Each one of us has the capacity to dream and the ability to create dreams the size of Mt. Everest. Our visions transform those dreams into journeys that can take us from our present state of existence to the marvelous destinations in our future.

The key to all of this is believing in your ability to make those dreams come true! Hold fast to your dreams and believe in your ability to reach the impossible.

## Our Ancestors Were Dreamers

It's amazing how black people of the past dreamed dreams and reached goals with practically no resources. For years my father's mother eked out a living as a Bel Air, Maryland domestic making five dollars a week. As a single parent, Carrie Copeland Brown (or Nanny Carrie as I knew her) raised two sons, saw my father, Wilson Copeland, graduate from college in 1941, remarried, and took her life savings to purchase a home. All as a five-dollar-a-week-maid.

So many African Americans can share that same story of transforming humble beginnings into a lifetime of sacrificial achievement. Look at the nickels, dimes and pennies raised to start most of the Historically Black Colleges and Universities. Janitors, street sweepers, cooks and maids dared to dream the impossible and paved the way for their children to someday capture the American dream.

So the next time you complain about not having a second pair of designer jeans; stop, count your blessings, and be thankful for the five-dollar-a-week cooks, maids and janitors of your own cultural heritage whose sacrifices made it possible for you to achieve success.

## Starting A Dream Box

Before you finish this book, I want you to start a "Dream Box." Use any box around your home, or buy a new one  This will be a special storage place for pictures, articles, words, wish lists, or miniature items that resemble a future purchase or goal. What will you put in your DREAM BOX? Will you load it with lofty, unattainable items, or will you pack it with possibilities, plans and future dates that will plant the seeds of your future?

When I started my new home dream box in 1995, I didn't censor my imagination. I loaded that box with pictures from 7,000 square foot luxury homes to cozy bungalows nestled between the trees of familiar city streets. You see your dream box should capture the breadth of your possibilities including all the opportunities that you can possibly achieve. Want to buy a new home? Want to send your kids to college? Want to have the financial freedom to care for your aging parents? Want to easily give money to that new community center that must be built? Start with your dream box.

It's all up to you and it all starts with you. Your dream box is waiting to be filled with your creativity, your possibilities, and the plans of your future.

## From Dream to Reality

In 1995 I started my dream box and filled it with magazines, books, pictures, and articles on building a new home. I set a goal to become a homeowner in five years or less. I visited new construction sites, and trekked through Sunday open houses just to see what was on the market. Achieving that gigantic goal of building a house was about as far-fetched as you can possibly imagine. I was recently divorced with three teenagers to feed. As a struggling small business owner my cash flow was in constant flux. My "new house" savings account totaled less than $100. And the college tuition bills for my oldest child were always right around the corner. As impossible as my dream of home ownership seemed, I never stopped dreaming about building a new home.

What seems unimaginable can turn into reality when your faith, your commitment to your career or business, and your determination to turn the corner in your life empowers you to achieve the impossible.

With the help of loving family members, countless prayers, focusing on my business, and that dream box, I built my new home in 2001. I was only one year off from my original goal deadline. The thrill of my life came when I watched my house being built. Those six months of construction magic were some of the most joyous I've had.

You too can start a dream box that can be filled with the aspirations and ambitions of your future. Fill that dream box to the brim and cash in on the possibilities that are waiting for you.

Empowerment begins when you believe in yourself.

## Your Dream Box May Open Pandora's Box

When you start a dream box don't expect your friends and family members to immediately understand what you are doing. In fact expect them to sometimes become your chief critics. They mean no harm; they love you, and want to do whatever they can to protect you. But sometimes those closest to you don't have a clue about all of the possibilities bursting inside your spirit.

Sometimes when you're planning for your future or dreaming about what tomorrow will bring your way, you need to carefully share your plans with the right people. During the early stages of creating your dreams, you should only share your thoughts with the most supportive friends, colleagues, and family members. They may not understand why you are planning certain things, but will remain encouraging and supportive of your aspirations.

So step out of faith, pick and choose your supporters, and dream on about the excitement of your future.

## Self Sabotage

You look around and you're the culprit who's opened up the Pandora's box of your doubts, fears, and hesitations.

Stop sabotaging your dreams. It's the negative self-talk that stops you cold when you're on a roll in turning the corner on your own circumstances. You know the drill, you're on your job and others are making more money than you are, but you talk yourself out of asking for that raise. You figure that there must be something secretly wrong with your job performance, and slowly your inner doubt and negative self-talk turns into frustration, resentment, and anger toward others.

You dream of a beautiful home that you will own, transforming you from a lifetime renter into a confident and creative homeowner. But you let life's daily obstacles trip you up, and suddenly you find yourself farther and farther away from that picket fence, two car garage, and finished basement of your dreams.

Stop stealing your personal dreams and start planning for tomorrow morning when you can turn those dreams into reality.

## Your Accountability Team

Real friends are worth pure gold. They're with you when you're up, and hold you up when you're down. The best way to climb your ladder of success is by finding a small group of people who you can call your "Empowerment Accountability Team." These are your trusted girlfriends who call you out when your ego gets out of control. These are the tried and true guyfriends who pull your coattails when you're full of yourself. This small group of angels gives you the support you need when everything possible has gone wrong on your job. And if you're still looking for work, your team encourages you to keep the faith by not giving up. They are there for you, and alert you to signs of insecurity, self-doubt and fear that may sabotage the possibilities of your dream box.

Everybody needs an accountability team. It's rarely more than five or six people who should be a part of your personal circle of support.

Pick them carefully, and don't limit your selection to just family members. Value them, respect them and listen to their advice when you know deep down inside they're telling you the truth.

Change your accountability team when the combination of trusted advisors no longer meets your needs. You'll know when this change should happen if you're veering off course and your team can't guide you back on track.

You don't have to meet with your accountability team as a group. Perhaps you can call them on the phone to review a new idea, a new course of action, or a future purchase. Your accountability team can be as formally structured or as loosely arranged as you see fit.

Stop thinking about who you will select for your accountability team and simply call up your trusted friends and get one started.

## From a Vision to a Dream to a Goal

In order to fulfill your vision you ultimately must create goals. Those goals are best created when you establish a road map to chart the direction you'll take to reach your goals.

A road map can be created on a piece of paper, in a notebook, or in a palm pilot. Your road map should be broken down into months, weeks and days and can include the details of reaching your goals and the timing it will take to get there. It should also indicate possible roadblocks, obstacles, detours and setbacks you anticipate before they actually occur. If you want to start or expand your investment portfolio or savings plan, your roadmap would include the steps needed to establish and maintain a financial plan that will keep you on course. If a new home is on the horizon your roadmap should include the costs associated with purchasing this home, a specific timeline you'll need to save the money, and the actual date you plan on closing on your new home.

I still have the 1995 postcard picturing the home I wanted to buy and the timeframe I planned on purchasing that home: 2000. From a mere dream to an actual goal, I closed on my home in March 2001. This process now serves as a powerful reminder that the power of suggestion, a roadmap, and a plan of action will help you reach those goals.

Do whatever it takes to successfully reach your goals by setting up a roadmap that will direct your path of personal fulfillment.

## Goal Setting - One Week at a Time

Work on your goals one week at a time. Go back and add up all of this week's accomplishments. Don't fret over what didn't get finished, because you can start next week's list with those items. Did you finish that report at work? Help your children with their homework? Finish that weekend renovation project you've put off for the last few months? No matter how big or small the project or task, write down exactly what you've accomplished.

Now look at all of the leftover items, prioritize them, and create your goal sheet for next week. Whatever must get finished becomes your number one priority. And those projects that will take a bit more time will move down a notch or two.

While you're working on that list, begin to think of WHO can help you reach your goals. Can your children help you out? Or your spouse or significant other? What about a co-worker or staff member? Perhaps someone in your neighborhood, community group, church or temple can lend a hand. Is it possible that your accountability team can give you moral support?

Whatever it takes, YOU have the power to reach your goals by working on them one week at a time.

## Set Your Goals and Celebrate Baby Victories

A great way to signal progress is by celebrating your baby victories. They're the small milestones that seem insignificant, yet ultimately make the difference between success and failure.

Your boss is interested in your new ideas and begins to show you a new level of respect. That's a victory. For the first time ever friends and colleagues start asking you for your opinion on important matters. That's a victory. Your teenagers are actually listening to you this time. That's a victory. A new opportunity opens up for you to make extra money. That's a victory.

Stop long enough to celebrate the little breakthroughs that are popping up as you create the dreams of your future. Embrace them and expect many more like them as you choose to build a better life for yourself, your family, and all of the people connected to you.

## Ready, Aim, Focus!

There are 1001 distractions that can keep you from reaching your goals. You started on track with your goal setting plan and had enough enthusiasm to beat the band. Then you got side-tracked watching your neighbor, co-worker or good friend move just a bit ahead of you. Now you're all bent out of shape. Your emotions have taken over and now you find yourself as the number one spectator in someone else's parade.

What's the answer? Focus on you. Only you. And most importantly you. Sincerely congratulate that other person when they succeed, but don't let your own insecurities sabotage the very plan that will take you to the top.

## Believe In Your Vision.
### Create Your Dream Box.
### Believe In Your Goals.

It's amazing to see the shock and surprise on the faces of TV game show contestants after they've just won a cool million dollars. They can't believe their good fortune, even though they've beaten the odds often by spending endless nights studying trivia questions in

_____

# *Have you ever*

been knocked down

for a full eight count?

Pick yourself up and

keep stepping.

_____

preparation for their big TV appearance. They set a goal of winning and when their dream comes through, they can't believe it's really happening.

Are you like those winning game show contestants working hard to reach your goals, only to end up in disbelief when you actually get there?

It's often been said that the fear of success is more frightening than the fear of failure.

Celebrate your success, get the shock off your face, and tell yourself that you truly deserve to achieve the goals that you've visualized, dreamed about, and are now working hard to accomplish.

## The Rugged Road to Personal Achievement

Have you ever been knocked down for a full eight count?

Pick yourself up and keep stepping. Step toward your aspirations. Step through your fears and weaknesses. Grab hold of a *Higher Power* and master your universe step by step.

So often it is through the stillness of our failures that we achieve our greatest victories. Life knocks you down to your lowest point when everything seems to come crashing down around you. Then suddenly, glimmers of hope, encouragement and opportunity whisper to you to get up and keep on stepping.

That's how we learn to take the bitter with the sweet. We learn humility in the midst of our challenges. And we find new ways to rise above our circumstances as we aim for a brighter tomorrow.

So pick yourself up, dust yourself off, and always remember that you DO have what it takes to press forward by finding the possibilities of your future.

---

# *Prepare yourself*

for the troubles in your life

by arming yourself with

the energy, faith, and attitude

to fully confront your issues,

both good and bad, each day.

---

## CHAPTER THREE

# Getting Through the Storms of Life

Who said you weren't going to have troubles in life? The only people who are trouble-free are in cemeteries, resting peacefully in their eternal home. The rest of us are still on the battleground of life.

Prepare yourself for the troubles in your life by arming yourself each day with the energy, faith, and attitude to fully confront your issues, both good and bad. Start your day with meditation or prayer, recite positive affirmations, and embrace the wacky world that awaits you.

Remember that everyone has a season of troubles. Yours may be today and your neighbor's tomorrow. What's important is to stay focused and clear on the guiding principles that constitute who you are. With that reality, you'll stay on course and you'll become a strong positive individual.

## Family Joy - Family Pain

Life teaches you that the collection of our experiences bundled together with the tear-soaked rags of our joys and sorrows make up the patchwork quilt of our existence. That wouldn't have made any sense to me during my relatively carefree teenage years, or even during the days of my early 20's when I thought I could conquer the world.

25

But now in my middle years I can touch and feel the tattered fabric that makes me who I am.

I'll be the first to admit that life is hard. It's extraordinarily exhilarating and hard at the same time. One day you've figured out the puzzles of your universe, and the next day the puzzle you've so carefully assembled shatters into a thousand tiny pieces. You take a deep breath, repair as many puzzle pieces as you can, and discover that it's impossible to recreate the pieces of your past. In some cases you must resort to finding new pieces to make it all work.

## Painful Puzzles of My Past

The events of 1997 reshaped my life in such a dramatic way, that the residual effects tug at my heart and routinely leave me aching with anguish and sadness.

I am the mother of three children. I wear the motherhood title like a badge of honor. My children are my life, and I wouldn't trade anything for the joy that they've brought me. And with that joy has come the never-ending dirty diapers, colic, crying, sibling fights, laughter, punishments, close calls, and proud moments that remind me of my nurturing past.

## Lorna

My oldest daughter is Lorna, a beautiful young woman in her mid-twenties who wants to capture that American dream. She visualizes a promising career as a clinical psychologist, a home straight out of a designer's magazine, a handsome husband who's smart and resourceful, and a child for each spare bedroom in the house. Lorna knew that she wanted to attend Spelman College when she was nine years old, and she set out on an academic course to achieve that goal. I didn't realize that she had a one-track college mind until she had returned from the "Black College" tour in her junior year of high school. She stomped the campus grounds of several well-known colleges during that trip and applied to a few of them during that frenetic time in her senior year. Lorna also applied to predominately white schools, and received scholarship offers from schools eager to take her on. But she held out for Spelman to make her an offer. Day after day in the spring of her senior year she'd race to the front door, checking to see if that thick packet had come from the all-women's college in Atlanta. A thick envelope offered you the keys to the campus. A thin envelope meant instant rejection. The school hadn't accepted you.

When that day came in mid-March, 1994 she could hardly believe her eyes. Thick envelope. Spelman College. Addressed to Lorna A. Thomas. "Congratulations. On behalf of the Dean of Admissions of Spelman College we welcome you to the class of 1998." She nailed it. Her grand prize. The biggest puzzle piece of her young life. A dream fulfilled.

It was so satisfying to see my oldest daughter so happy and so excited about the years ahead of her on the campus of Spelman. I could hardly contain my joy as the mother of a budding Spelmanite. As her final months of high school seemed to fly by—she was inducted into the National Honor Society, served out her term as senior class treasurer, and graduated as one of the outstanding students of Milton High School in Milton, Massachusetts.

Helping people was always a life goal for Lorna. With a strong aptitude for science, Lorna decided to major in psychology with a pre-med minor. Her early aspirations included a possible career as a pediatrician. I couldn't be happier, and I admit that part of me lived vicariously in her shadows. I had wanted to become a doctor as a teen, but diverted to music. High school chemistry torpedoed my plans to achieve medical greatness.

Lorna excelled in college, fell in and out of love, and in her senior year became a member of the sorority of her mother, grandmother and aunt: Delta Sigma Theta Sorority. I've watched her through the years and marvel at what she has become—a hardworking and sensitive young woman who can never be fooled by hypocritical nonsense.

After graduating from Spelman, Lorna worked with a research organization while deciding whether or not medical school was in her future. Her plans changed and a career in psychology became her passion. As this book was being published, Lorna was finishing her coursework at the University of Hartford and sinking her teeth into her dissertation. Her plan is to receive her doctorate in clinical psychology over the next two years and help young minority youth with self-esteem issues.

## Michelle

Michelle is my child of great amazement. Three years younger than Lorna, she's been surprising since the day she was born. The last born in our family, Michelle often behaves like a middle child, struggling to find her place in society. She prides herself at being different and makes a point not to follow the crowd. She's a self-starter and the most punctual one in the family. School has always been a challenge to Michelle; but she could easily be a poster girl for courage, determination and tenacity. She never gives up, no matter how hard the task. I remember Michelle's classic response to family and friends when asked what she wanted to become as a grownup. "A doctor and a dancer," declared Michelle with the confidence of a forward-thinking nine-year-old child. It pleased me to know that my lifeline, that extension of my existence, my children, had such high hopes and aspirations for themselves. To hear Michelle talk of her dreams anchored the validation of my parenting skills. And it's been her determination and perseverance that has taken Michelle through the difficulties in her young life.

Like most children, Michelle has explored many career options since those days of choosing doctoring and dancing. Her schooling has been one of her chief sources of exploration, trials, and tribulation. Yet school has been a struggle for Michelle, making her path a more difficult life course than her sister's. Michelle is three years younger than Lorna, and in many ways they're worlds apart. Loving, yes. Sisters, yes. But different styles, tastes, and habits.

As the family introvert, when early challenges hit her, it was her silence that masked the problems she faced. For example, completing homework assignments sometimes felt like climbing a mountain blindfolded. Reading comprehension was a key stumbling block and affected the years Michelle would struggle to get decent grades and simply pass exams. She was relegated to the reading resource room early in life — those federally funded school programs known as Chapter 766 in Massachusetts. The years that she was assigned to that special educational track created a stigma that has remained with Michelle to this day. She was a resource room student from first grade through middle school.

One day she just wanted out. Michelle needed the extra help in strengthening her educational foundation but ultimately grew to resent the forced assignment to Chapter 766. Being removed from her regular classroom for certain times of the week had left its mark on her self-esteem. It began to define who she was in her own eyes and that of her classmates. To some extent that experience has remained inside of Michelle's core being—defining who she is and what the world says of her limitations and strengths.

But her story doesn't stop there. My Michelle is a resilient young woman whose strengths far outweigh her weaknesses. She is one of the most punctual people on the planet. She'll show up for work or school regardless of the weather conditions or other circumstances life brings her way. Her timeliness is well known, so much so that Lorna and I still rely on her early morning long distance wake-up calls when we need the extra boost. She was always my first child to get up on school days and often the first student in class. While working summer jobs, Michelle figured out how to get to her job on time and how to arrange her social activities so she would be well ahead of the crowd.

My fondest memories take me back to Michelle's Girl Scout cookie days. What a crackerjack salesperson she was. As a youngster she identified her target market (classmates, teachers, and church members), sold her cookies, collected every penny and delivered every box, all by herself. I helped very little and stood back in amazement at what this ball of energy could do on her own. Each year she ranked as one of the top sellers in her troop.

Today Michelle continues to define her path as a young woman making her way in the world. Michelle works full-time while working on her undergraduate degree part-time at Chicago State University as a transfer student. Flashbacks of the resource room haven't stopped her from charging through difficult courses and passing her classes. She's had many ups and downs but has pulled up her grade point average with remarkable skill and perseverance. Michelle is a survivor and has found an inner toughness that will take her far in life.

I'll never forget the day Michelle announced to the family that she was going to become a chef. We applauded her choice and visualized the delicious meals she'd create at the restaurant bearing her name. She's still pursuing that dream and plans on attending cooking school when she graduates from college. I believe she'll reach her goal. Michelle has demonstrated mental toughness that will help her endure whatever comes her way.

Michelle is a living example of discovering the strength that ultimately comes from our struggles. She should know. She has been forced to struggle through the difficulty of living in the spirit of Mikey.

## Mikey

Mikey is Michelle's twin brother. Mickarl Darius Thomas, Jr., Mikey, as he was affectionately called, born 20 minutes before his sister, displayed the exuberance and gregariousness of an active boy the minute he was born.

It's a surreal experience having twins, especially for someone like me who always looked at mothers of twins as such odd people.

They were women who seemed like superproducers, populating the planet like production carriers determined to out-pace the others bringing forth life on the planet. Then I became one of those odd people populating the planet and spitting out two for the price of one.

I'll never forget those early spring days in 1979. Already aware of my pregnancy, my husband and I were delighted with having another baby. Lorna was such a delightful two-year-old with chubby cheeks and an affectionate demeanor. I looked forward to delivering another bundle of joy sometime during the lazy days of that summer.

I trotted off to Dallas that spring to attend my Mary Kay Cosmetics business conference and remember the accepting glances of those who guessed how far along I was in my pregnancy. When I returned from Dallas, I nonchalantly checked in with my doctor for my routine maternity visit and remember her cool demeanor transforming to a bit of concern. As her eyes widened she said, "You're awfully large to be in your fourth month. We'd better order an ultrasound for you." I didn't panic, and merely thought I was going to have a very big baby.

My denial continued as I lay on the table during my ultrasound and watched with amazement as the technician located the first baby resting comfortably in a sea of fluids. That turned out to be Mikey. With a gooey substance spread on my expanded stomach, the technician zigzagged his medical probe on my abdomen in search for more buried treasure. After some time, down in the depths of my uterus he spotted her dancing away. Another baby moving to the beat of its own drummer. It was Michelle.

I lay on the table in shock as the technician conferred with my doctor to confirm his findings. "Congratulations, Mrs. Thomas. You're going to have twins!"

## Only Odd People Have Twins

Not me, I thought! Only those odd people who overpopulate the world had multiple births. I'm not one of those odd people. Slowly the realization hit me that I was indeed going to deliver two babies in the summer of 1979.

Mikey and Michelle made their grand entrance into St. Francis Hospital in Norristown, Pennsylvania August 7, 1979. Thankfully my mother and mother-in-law were there to rescue two young parents unprepared for the joys and sorrows of raising not two children, but three.

Now there was Lorna, Mikey and Michelle. I'll never forget Lorna's first reaction when the twins were brought home from the hospital. As two tightly wrapped bundles were dramatically paraded through our front door three-year old Lorna quietly asked, "Where are they going to sleep?" Once she felt comfortable with our answer she quickly assumed the role of big sister, a role she faithfully plays to this day.

## The Mirror-Opposite Twin

Just as Michelle was the introvert, Mikey was the extrovert. His social skills matched his intellect; he was talkative and mischievous. You could always count on Mikey creating mayhem around the house, and he never ceased to taunt his sisters whenever he got the chance. He loved his sisters and needed to remind them that as the only boy in the house it was his department to create a little trouble from time to time.

One of those moments occurred when Mikey decided that Michelle needed a haircut to match the styles of her doll collection. We've all heard that twins have a special bond, and sometime it's expressed in strange ways. Michelle seemed to give in to her brother, even when it wasn't in her best interest.

I was out of town. Their dad was working at home in another room when Mikey, with scissors in hand, chopped off Michelle's beautiful bangs, leaving a clump of thick dark brown hair on the floor. For whatever reason, it didn't seem to bother Michelle until her misfortune was reported to her father. After a tense moment of horror at my child with the mangled hairstyle, Michelle burst into tears while Mikey tried to shrink away from the scene of the crime.

He was just like that. A natural prankster, full of energy and mischief. His natural shenanigans got him into real trouble in his junior year of high school when a fight with a school chum could have landed him in trouble with the police if the parents of his friend not had mercy on his impulsiveness.

Mikey was very smart and had very keen analytical skills. A strong test taker, he was allowed to take the SAT exam for the first time as a twelve-year-old. That served as preparation for his future. He took it a second time later in high school. He was also a very popular boy at school, in the neighborhood, and at our church.

The bumps and bruises in life never deterred my son to show respect for his elders. As a preacher's kid, Mikey and his sisters spent a fair amount of time in church, social gatherings, national conventions, and local fundraisers. He and his sisters had been trained to greet the public with grace and friendliness. Mikey developed a special type of charm that would disarm the most ferocious contrarian with the flash of his smile. He was an outgoing and loving child who loved sports, fast cars, and debating current events.

For many years Michelle towered over Mikey. Her lean angular body betrayed her shyness when she looked down on her twin brother for a word of advice. Mikey was shorter, but fit, and could swiftly outrun many of his bigger, bulkier friends. As they reached adolescence, their growth spurts evened out. By the time they reached their senior year in high school, Mikey and Michelle were about the same height.

## A Boy's Love of Sports

At an early age Mikey exhibited a natural talent for sports. A favorite picture of mine shows six-year-old Mikey in a white Tae Kwon Do suit ready to do battle with anyone who crossed his path. Mikey's athletic talent turned into a love of sports.

Through the years, little league baseball (Mikey played with his twin sister) transitioned to basketball and ultimately football. As one of the shortest members on his team, Mikey navigated his way onto the Canton Pop Warner Football Team. By the time he reached Milton High School he had grown in stature, perfected his game, and ultimately won a spot on the varsity football team.

## Team Vision Team Leadership

His skills paid off in his senior year when Mikey was selected as one of three co-captains of the football team, the Milton High Wildcats. The summer of 1996 was particularly important as he and his team warriors trained and strategized their season's game plan with Coach Riordan. They practiced throughout the hot August days, conditioned their bodies, and focused on a winning year. It was full speed ahead for the hometown team.

August turned to September and the season blasted off with high expectations. Everyone wanted a big win for the Wildcat's first game of the season. When it didn't happen, the team was cheered on to turn the first game's loss into a win for game two. It didn't happen at game two, three, four, five, or six. With a 0-6 season, the Milton Wildcats' popularity at school was waning. Classmates heckled the embattled football team while parents comforted the weekend warriors as they licked their wounds.

Throughout this tough season, the team never lost its spirit. It played on game after game like there was no tomorrow. To counteract the jeers at school, Mikey composed a heartfelt commentary for the school newspaper, urging the student body to hang in with the team. Many of the varsity players were new to the team, given that their seasoned players had graduated the year before.

Game six disappeared into game seven with another disappointing loss. In the end, the Milton Wildcats lost all eight games, including the Thanksgiving finale against rival Braintree High.

## The Spirit of Winning

It was the spirit of winning that kept those boys from losing their courage. They kept playing in spite of mounting losses. The three co-captains remained focused. The Coach firmly fixed on crafting a victory on the playing field. My son's newspaper commentary won him the kind of respect from students and teachers never before seen in the face of school defeat.

Those young men taught the community that the spirit of winning is more powerful than staggering defeat on the playing field. Each one of them had a winning attitude. It was their attitude; their determination to win made them a standout team. Yes, they lost all eight games, but they never lost their quest for victory. They had been conditioned to maintain a fiercely positive attitude in the midst of defeat. It was one of life's lessons for all of us to contemplate that earned Mikey the unsung hero award, the Daniel E. Duggan Trophy.

## The Twins Skip Through Their Senior Year

In the midst of stunning football defeats came the college application journey. What a process that was for me. Working with Lorna during her college application process was pretty straightforward on my part. One child. Several school choices. Complete one application at a time. But now the scenario was different. Two children. More school choices. At least two applications at a time.

The fall of 1996 was a jumble of football games, homework assignments, high school transcripts, and teacher recommendations, on top of countless community and church activities. Both Mikey and Michelle were active members of the church their father pastored, Charles Street African Methodist Episcopal in Roxbury, Massachusetts. Michelle served as a founding member of the Junior Trustee Board while Mikey served as the founding President of the Junior Steward Board. Like their older sister, the twins were active members of the South Shore Chapter of Jack and Jill, one of black America's mainline social organizations for young people. Michelle served as Secretary of the Jack and Jill Teen Group. And just like Lorna, Mikey led the Teen Group as its President. Serving in leadership roles was expected in our family. Despite the pressure to succeed, they stayed the course and continued to demonstrate their ability to succeed.

## The College Bound Twins

January 6, 1997 was a perfectly joyous day. It was a family moment like no other. Both twins were accepted to the colleges of their choice on the same day. Michelle learned that Tuskegee University in Tuskegee, Alabama had accepted her into the freshman class of 2001. And Mikey heard from his dream school, the only school he had applied to, Morehouse College, in Atlanta, Georgia.

I was thanking God that Tuskegee had accepted Michelle, knowing school was never easy for her, and taking standardized tests required the anguishing task of perseverance. With Michelle we selected a few "safety schools" in the event that rejection letters crossed our doorway, With Mikey there was only one application and one school, Morehouse. Yes, there were 237 invitations to apply to various colleges across the country, primarily because of his high school honors and high SAT scores. But years before he had identified Morehouse as his school of choice. His father had wanted him to attend that school.

The celebrations continued in April, 1997 when a surprise letter arrived, awarding Mikey a full four-year academic scholarship to Morehouse. "What a blessing!" I shouted. I'd have three kids in college and only be responsible for two tuition payments. I was a proud peacock showcasing my offspring who continued to deliver the goods.

## High School Graduation Day for the Twins

The day of great celebration came on June 8, 1997 when Michelle and Mikey graduated from Milton High School. It was a steamy Sunday afternoon, the culmination of a hectic season of school activities. In addition to my workshops, consultations and presentations, I made Michelle's prom dress, snapped endless photographs, and mailed off one hundred invitations for the twins' graduation party we had planned. I was so excited about my children attending their high school prom—looking so lovely with their prom dates anchored at their sides. Good news came back from the prom when Michelle landed in the Prom Court. She looked so beautiful all made up and draped in her custom-designed evening gown.

My 80-year old mother had flown in for the special occasion, and we laughed, joked, and marveled about how time had flown. Lorna had just finished her junior year at Spelman. My brother and sister-in-law's only child, Lauren Copeland, had just completed her first year at Spelman. Bringing up the rear were Mikey and Michelle who would dash off to Morehouse and Tuskegee.

The graduation was simply perfect. Nearly two hundred seniors donned mortarboard hats, tassels, and gowns. The school colors were in full parade with the boys wearing red gowns and the girls in white gowns. It was an outside ceremony. The weather couldn't have been better. Mikey and Michelle sat together, the red and white symbols of high school success. As her name was announced Michelle gracefully rose from her chair, marched to the town council selectman, and thankfully took her diploma.

For Mikey, the drama erupted as he neared the open-air stage. He danced up to the platform, grinned from ear to ear, grabbed his diploma, and unexpectedly threw his hands up in the air, triumphant that his high school days were finally over.

## Party Mania

The party back at our home was a joyous occasion. Almost one hundred people attended the festivities that day. Black, white,

Hispanic and Asian youngsters occupied every party space available. Adults looked on with pride and happiness.

Mikey and Michelle continued to party with their friends until they left for the high school's all night party, a popular activity designed to help the graduating seniors have fun one final time in the safety of the school's gymnasium.

## The Eve of the Storm

It became serene after that night. Monday flowed into Tuesday, and the rest of the week brought post graduation reflections and memories. In an unusual move, Mikey immediately began preparing his list for the many thank you notes he would have to write for the graduation gifts received.

Michelle, the essence of punctuality, was already involved in writing her notes.

Lorna, Michelle, and Mikey engaged in deep discussions. They debated about sports and talked about the college days ahead of them. They bonded as only brothers and sisters can bond, having fun, teasing each other, laughing, and squeezing in an occasional hug.

They also made sure that my mother, "Grandma Copeland," was well taken care of as our very special houseguest.

For years my mother traveled from my hometown of Detroit, for extended visits with her clan in Massachusetts. We looked forward to every one of those visits. This one had been special for each one of us, and we welcomed her presence, her humor, and her elderly dignity.

Ignoring the superstitions of the date, I looked forward to Friday, June 13, 1997, because it was the day of the final party at our home. The South Shore Jack and Jill Teen Group held its graduation party at our house. About a dozen young people attended with younger siblings and parents in tow. The evening was a big hit. Our guests were entertained inside and out. The music flowed and the barbecue chicken, hotdogs and hamburgers never ran out. My image of Mikey teaching one of the young boys how to aim and fire a basketball in the hoop will never leave my mind.

## A Night of Tragedy

The Jack and Jill Party ended in much fanfare. Mikey and Lorna left later that evening to attend the birthday party of a family friend just fifteen minutes from our home. Michelle bowed out and decided to stay home that evening.

At 21, Lorna, a pretty steady driver, drove the two of them to the party in my mini-van. Most of the party guests were young professionals over the age of 21. Alcohol was served at the party.

Lorna later recalls a philosophical conversation she had with her brother that evening. He asked her about college, what to expect, and how the academic environment had treated her over the past two years. They talked on despite the music, fanfare and dancing in their midst.

I had given Mikey permission to spend the night at the home of the birthday honoree. Lorna prepared to leave her brother in the safe care of the family friends she had known most of her life. As she prepared to leave, she lightly squeezed her brother, so as not to embarrass him in front of pretty girls and macho young men.

He rejected the light embrace and wanted a great big hug from his older sister. An odd request, Lorna thought, but she complied anyway and received the bear hug of her life from her brother. It would be their last. Before getting in her car, Mikey shouted, "I love you!" Lorna lovingly returned the affection.

She returned home in the wee hours of Saturday June 14, 1997. I had just gone to bed, since an unusual burst of urgent energy had forced me to clean up my house before going to sleep.

Lorna pampered herself with a manicure. She heard the telephone ring at 4:30 a.m. It was Rev. Gracie Redfearn, one of the ministers from Charles Street AME. Her message was grim. Her nephew, a Boston police officer, had just left the scene of a terrible single occupant automobile accident. He knew the victim, and it had shaken him to his core.

Lorna dropped the phone and came racing up the stairs, choking back the tears of a nightmare. "Mom! There's been a terrible accident. It's Mikey! He GONE! We have to pick him up at the morgue!"

I couldn't believe my ears. This was a nightmare that was not supposed to happen. How could my lovable, living son be dead? He was alive only hours ago.

By now my house erupted into pandemonium, with screams, and wails coming from the entire second floor. My mother, slowed by age, was dancing a circled death dance. Michelle was crying, angry and yelling at the walls. Lorna was shedding uncontrollable tears of grief. And I resembled the women of the Middle East. I wailed, screamed and joined my mother in her death dance. It was awful. It was not supposed to happen. But it was very real.

## What Actually Happened

My son, like thousands of teenagers drank alcohol and smoked marijuana with his friends to be part of the "in" crowd. I did not know this. I now realize that under-age drinking impacts families all over the globe.

After Lorna left the party Mikey started drinking and decided to go joy riding. He was a new driver, and had only received his driver's license two months earlier. He had passed his driver's test. Michelle had failed hers.

Impulsively, Mikey picked up a set of car keys left on the table by one of the party guests. He decided to test out the green BMW he had admired for weeks before the party. This friend had actually allowed Mikey to drive his car a few weeks before. In the darkness of that quiet Boston street, Mikey became the indestructible teenager so many of us became at that age.

He raced down the street. Turned the car around and raced up a steep hill. By this time the partygoers heard the car, realized that Mikey and the car keys were gone and begin chasing after him.

The timing was too little, too late. Mikey lost control of the fast car while climbing that hill. The car reached the top of the hill, sped downward, veered to the right and slammed into a retaining wall at 60 miles per hour. Even though one of the party guests was an off-duty police officer skilled in CPR, the crash defeated any rescue efforts he attempted. Fire fighters were on the scene in record time, to no avail. Mickarl Darius Thomas, Jr. was pronounced dead at the scene.

The street that claimed his life ironically was the namesake of his beloved older sister: Lorna Road. An autopsy report would later confirm Mikey's blood alcohol level had been almost twice the legal limit. He was 17 years old.

## Death and Its Aftermath

Losing my son put me face to face with the level of pain, suffering and grief only a parent could face when losing a child in sudden death. A whole new world was opening up to me, and I wanted no part of it. Making the phone call to the children's father was horrific. As the sun began to rise on that eerily beautiful day I knew my world had changed forever. Literally hundreds of people streamed through my house for a solid week. Friends flew in from around the country. One friend and colleague left a meeting in London to attend Mikey's funeral.

The Boston Globe and Quincy Patriot Ledger paid tribute to a good boy who died too soon. Thomas Menino, the mayor of Boston, called me to extend his condolences.

My experience had transitioned from buying party balloons to picking out caskets and cemetery plots.

## The Funeral for All People

My son was dead and my life seemed over. The joy of raising my children had suddenly turned to ash.

By Thursday, June 19, 1997, the gravity of my new life as a grieving mother had taken its toll. I hadn't eaten for almost a week, yet…I had the ultimate test of facing a mid-morning crowd of mourners who would be gathering at Charles Street to say goodbye to my Mikey.

# GETTING THROUGH THE STORMS

The number of people who had turned out for my son's funeral overwhelmed me. The church could comfortably seat nearly 500 people. That number was nearly doubled outside in the streets. Police officers on horseback had come. Visiting dignitaries had come. Ministers from across the country had come. It seemed like the world had come to say goodbye to this remarkable young man.

As I sat in my numbness on the front pew looking over a casket filled with flowers, teddy bears, and tears, I couldn't believe what was happening. It wasn't until I witnessed the 108 students from Milton High School march past the casket that my spirit began to soar. They were three busloads strong; Black, white, Hispanic and Asian. Teenagers, classmates, football buddies, friends, administrators, and teachers. All there to say goodbye.

I realized that my life was not over—just beginning from a new perspective. I realized that I had an important job to fulfill, to live my life for the purpose of empowering others to succeed. I had a new responsibility to help these young people cope with the loss of their friend. I needed to guide my daughters through the treacherous waters of their own guilt, pain, and suffering from the loss of their beloved Mikey.

I was needed in a new dynamic way to help bring hope to those whose personal challenges seemed overwhelming.

---

# *Don't surrender*

to the trials and tribulations

of today. Claim the victory and

set sail for a better tomorrow.

---

# CHAPTER FOUR

# Mental Toughness

## Learning What You Do and Do Not Control

The world stood anguishingly still when my 17 year old son was killed in that 1997 automobile accident. He graduated from high school and was buried in his grave within eleven short days.

Mikey left behind a twin sister, an older sister, grieving parents, and a world filled with saddened hearts. I thought my life couldn't go on without him. That summer of 1997 was the first time I realized how much of life I didn't control.

You know you're on your road to empowerment when you begin to understand that so much of life is out of your control. What you do control is your attitude and your perspective on life. I learned that painful summer that death had claimed my son, but life still triumphed in my two beautiful living daughters, Lorna and Michelle. Ever since that fateful time I treat each day as a gift from God—a gift to enjoy with the wondrous potential of a positive attitude.

What attitude do you bring into your life? Will the pain of your past throw a blanket on your tomorrow? Or will you stand up, brush yourself off and let the energy of a positive attitude propel you toward your future? Will you fully live through life's challenges? That choice ultimately is yours.

## What Do You Say When a Young Person Dies?

When the worst nightmare DOES happen involving the death of a young person what do you say that appropriate, caring and thoughtful? When my son died in 1997 so many friends went silent because they just didn't know what to say.

Well first of all unless you have lost a child, don't say "I know how you feel," because you really don't! And please don't say, "you'll get over it." It's not like losing your parents or close friends. The death of a child is in a category all by itself.

What you can say is, "I'll be here for you whenever you want to talk." or "I'm a good listener, and even though I can't exactly feel your pain, I'm opening my heart and soul to you whenever you need me."

The love of my family and the unwavering support of my friends helped get me through the most difficult days of my life. Lend a listening ear, watch what you say, and be there for that parent who's living through the death of a child.

## Life is Not Fair

Life is not fair and evil is present everywhere. Life owes you nothing. You have to find a quality life for yourself with your own skills, your own faith, and your own support system.

It sounds depressing but it's true. And only when you fortify your personal empowerment will you find the path that will help you navigate the pitfalls of life. Empowerment doesn't take away your troubles. It gives you that competitive edge to fight on when life isn't fair to you! It's that unending faith that gives you the strength to do the impossible when others have written you off as a total failure.

Yes, life is not fair but you can still dare to be different when you defy the odds and capture the essence of your purpose on the planet. Be realistic, but never stop dreaming. Face your fears, but stretch beyond yourself at the same time. Shape your thoughts, control your attitude, and live the life you were meant to embrace.

## Moving Through - Not Moving On

As modern day professionals we get up, go to work, come home, handle family responsibilities, find free time for ourselves, go to bed and start the cycle all over again the next day. So when setbacks and tragedies strike, we are often paralyzed in bewilderment, confusion, and fear desperately needing to resume some sense of "normalcy."

Anyone who has survived a life and death crisis will tell you that your life can never be the same and you learn to move through your circumstances as opposed to moving on. You painfully learn to accept the things you cannot change while handling your emotions that often become inflamed in flashbacks at a moment's notice.

Moving through the storms of life is different from artificially moving on. It teaches us all that the delicate journey of life expands well beyond our carefully scripted daily habits and rituals.

## Victim or Victor?

When are you going to stop being a victim and start becoming a victor?

Believe it or not, you're not the only person to suffer a major setback, lose a job, have family problems, rob Peter to pay Paul, or have health challenges. In life there's so much we'll never be able to control. But you can control the method you use to confront the problems that come into your life.

Victims surrender their emotions to their problems. Victors face their problems and figure out new ways to overcome the impossible.

So what will it be? Will you surrender or learn to become the victors of your challenges, trials, and tribulations? The choice is yours.

## Save Yourself

Life is waiting for you to save yourself. With God's help you can do the impossible. Need a bit of encouragement? Just read Joshua Chapter 1 Verses 1-9 from the Old Testament and turbo charge your path in life with new energy.

Save yourself and set a new course of action for your marriage, your family, your job, or important relationships.

Don't surrender to the trials and tribulations of today. Claim the victory and set sail for a better tomorrow.

Save yourself, empower yourself, crank up your faith, build up your fitness level, and get ready to blast off into new possibilities.

## Strength of Steel

It's the blazing heat that strengthens steel. My childhood field trips to the Ford Foundry in my hometown of Detroit taught me that. Men would take untreated metal and guide it through those fiery furnaces, making it tough enough to be shaped into an automobile frame. The noise and burst of flames always frightened me—but to see the end result was just short of remarkable.

What kind of fiery furnace is in store for you? Are you prepared to face the hot flames of your life so that your inner strength frames your tomorrows? It's those challenges, obstacles, problems, tragedies, and setbacks that really makes us tougher, even though they frighten us when they get too close.

Personal strength must be tested, just like steel gets tested before it becomes a car. Get ready for your tests and know that they are there to make you a stronger human being.

## Stand Up for Courage

There are times when I get frustrated and upset with the problems in my life. Trying to find my way out of tough financial or personal challenges can cause sleepless nights and never-ending days. But I find that there's always a little voice that keeps encouraging me to *stand* and resolve the problems. Without fail, solutions to my problems are never far away.

Do you know that solutions to your problems are never far away? If you throw up your hands and give up, you often push away the very answers that will resolve your dilemma. I suffer the same fears that you have and I know that when you face those fears and chip away at your problems, you're bound to solve most of them.

Find the courage to stand in the face of adversity. Use your problems as part of life's many lessons in finding patience, purpose, and persistence in forging ahead through tough times.

## Empowerment Secret: Expect the Unexpected

*It's time to stop being surprised about the unexpected!* Unexpected circumstances are life's realities put in motion to test our strength, our faith and our abilities to navigate through the storms that come our way. Your car breaks down just after you've paid all of your bills for the month. The roof leaks. Your child comes home with the worst report card ever. Your relationship that was supposed to last a lifetime is sinking fast. The doctor's office calls and needs to see you about your test results. You get a certified letter from the IRS.

Guard against the surprises that are bound to come your way by programming your mind to look for life's challenges. You are human and are bound to react to the unexpected. It's just *how* you frame your attitude that makes the difference.

So celebrate the good times and put on your emotional armor when the tough times creep in. You're going to make it through the best and worse of all your personal circumstances.

# *Pick your friends wisely*

at work and spread

your allegiances all

throughout your organization.

Your co-worker today could

be your boss tomorrow.

## CHAPTER FIVE

# *Empowerment Through Career Advancement*

### The Truth About Job Security

How focused are you on your career development? Don't tell me that you're completely relying on the good intentions of your employer. The days of job security are gone. It's up to *you* to take charge of your job and plan accordingly for a future of opportunities and challenges alike.

I remember over ten years ago explaining the importance of taking charge of your career to a group of disbelieving corporate executives. My message was too radical for them to hear at the time. But that same company since has gone through several mergers and laid off hundreds of workers—just as I had predicted in my past presentation to them. The call to action is a clear now as it was a decade ago. Know where you stand in your company, take nothing for granted, and keep an updated resume in your top drawer.

So take charge, stay focused and manage the growth and success path that is destined for you.

## Job Layoff: It Can Happen To You

Be prepared for the next round of job layoffs by staying on top of your career landscape. Economic cycles often forecast what jobs will make it and which ones could get eliminated. World events such as the September 11$^{th}$ terrorist attack, the 2003 War in Iraq, and a soft economy are increasingly impacting the stability of the worldwide job market.

Is your resume up to date? Are you ready to spring into action if the pink slips start landing on your company's doorstep? What plan do you have in place if your job is suddenly in jeopardy?

Whenever the economy is uncertain, take nothing for granted, and do whatever you must to prepare yourself for the possibility of a sudden career change. Keep up with company news, update your resume, and build new alliances with decision-makers who can help you if your job ends up on the chopping block. And don't forget to sharpen up your networking skills in order to connect with people who can help your career path.

## Stronger as a Team

It's amazing what lessons we can learn in the midst of having fun. That thought smacked me over the head when I took my turn paddling down the Kennebec River in beautiful Maine during a recent white water rafting trip. While riding out the big waves, I realized that the success of that very wet experience was not largely based on what I did alone, but what I did in connection with my nine other raft-mates.

Together we paddled, dodged the big rocks, and enjoyed a splash or two for the full 16-mile trip. It took all of us to make it work.

If one person fell out of the raft, we were all responsible for making sure that person got back in safely.

So much in life is like that white water rafting trip. We empower ourselves through the collective paddling down the river of life. We will make it when we learn to stick together, and pull each other up when we fall in.

## Balancing Work and Family

The old saying goes, "All work and no play makes Jack or Jill a dull boy or girl." The pace of our lives has exponentially exploded into overscheduling, overextensions, and non-stop overdrive. You may find yourself focusing on the expectations of your supervisor without regard for the 80-hour workweeks you're piling up.

If this sounds like you, my advice is to work hard on the job but don't do it at the expense of ruining your health or alienating your family.

The 1980's image of Superwoman or Superman no longer fits in the context of the 21st century. Have you trained your family to help you keep up the house in order for you to work hard for your paycheck each week? Even very young children can be taught the importance of picking up their clothes and helping out around the house. At work find new ways to team up with the right colleagues who can share the workload with you without compromising your personal productivity.

Find the right balance between work and family and live life to the fullest as you empower yourself to grow both on and off the job.

## Personal Networking

Empowered professionals understand that it's not who you know; it's who knows you that counts in life. How many people could put in a good word or two about you as decisions are being make about career advancement at your organization? How have you networked on and off the job by establishing your image as a trustworthy, responsible team-oriented individual?

Personal empowerment gives you permission to appropriately use self-promotion techniques that will give you brownie points on your career success path. The next time you do something positive for a boss or colleague that deserves extra attention, ask that a letter of recognition be sent directly to your personnel file. The more people know of your good work, the better your chances of moving up on the job. And it's even better when your good work can be documented in a letter or memo stating in detail why you're such a rock solid employee.

Success will come your way when you network effectively to build your image as the employee who's making a difference with confidence and connections.

## Spread Your Allies Around Your Office

When the marketplace is uncertain and workforce stability is threatened, you don't want to put all of your eggs in one basket. Pick your friends wisely at work and spread your allegiances strategically throughout your organization. Your co-worker today could be your boss tomorrow, or vice versa. Sometimes even the best boss can fall out of favor with senior management. This can leave you vulnerable if you've built up too much loyalty with just one person.

Take the time to get to know the other players in your organization. Know which way the wind will blow if a shake-up scatters people to the outer perimeters of your company. Do favors for people—it's a part of networking. Build relationships throughout your organization. It serves as a better safety net if you're department gets reshuffled.

Stay alert, know the players, and continue to take YOUR career into your own hands by building key relationships throughout your organization.

## How To Manage Your Boss

Too often a good worker is promoted to a management position, doesn't get properly trained, and ends up undermining the very employees he or she is charged to manage. If you become one of those victimized employees, don't sit back in corporate denial. Recognize that you're in a difficult workplace position and try to get some relief.

One solution is learning how to manage your boss. Assure your manager that you want to ensure his or her success. The better your on-the-job performance, the greater your boss will be recognized for developing his or her staff.

If a conflict develops between you and your supervisor, don't sit around and wait for the problem to go away. Can you have an honest conversation with your boss that will clear the air without getting you fired? Or can the human resource department delicately support you in your efforts? Figure out the most diplomatic and tactful way to resolve issues that will save face and save your career.

Managing your boss can be a tricky proposition if you're not strategic in your behavior. The last thing you want to do is intimidate your superior with accusations, confrontations, or activities that will sabotage your chances of future success.

One suggestion is to analyze your supervisor's management style. Is the person one who delegates assignments and leaves you alone to figure out the work all by yourself? Or is he/she a micro-manager who constantly hovers over your desk correcting every step of your project? Knowing how long your boss has been a manager is extremely important since it may easier to forge a new alliance with a less experienced person than a person who's been supervising for decades.

Assure your boss that you want the best for the team, and are sharpening up your technical skills in order to do your job more effectively.

Try to create quarterly or mid-year checkpoints so that you can compare your actual job performance with what your manager expects.

Believe in yourself and you can learn how to manage your boss. Cover your bases to ensure a positive outcome will surface from those sticky job-related challenges.

## Do Your Homework Before Your Interview

Don't miss out on landing that promising new job by pleading ignorant about not knowing anything about the company. Do your homework before you go on that important job interview. I often hear human resource professionals sigh in exasperation when candidate after candidate comes in for the interview, and knows next to nothing about the very company they want to join.

It's up to you to show how much you know about the history, focus, and line of business of the perspective company. Head to the nearest library and do an Internet search about the company or organization. If you don't know how to search the Internet, ask the reference librarian to help you. That's exactly what they are paid to do. And looking up recent newspaper and magazine articles will add more depth to your company research project.

Follow these tips, and you'll wow the interviewer with all of that new knowledge you've acquired as you work on getting that dream job that's waiting for you.

## Ingredients of a Great Résumé

When you've worked for your organization for longer than you care to remember you may not understand self-marketing 101. The best way to put forth your best *self* is with a compact, well written résumé.

A résumé is a snapshot of your work and educational history, constructed to show the best side of your skills, talents, performance, and accomplishments. There are hundreds of books that you can use as a reference as you update your résumé. Pick one or two and create sentences that use action verbs, and demonstrate your ability to problem solve while getting the job done efficiently.

Your résumé shouldn't extend beyond two pages. A one-page résumé is always preferred. Have another pair of eyes to proofread and edit your document, and get ready to net big results as you distribute your résumé to companies within your respective industry.

If you're not the best writer, hire trusted friend, business colleague, or a professional writer to help structure your résumé.

Sit down and list all of the positive traits of your life. Include your education, past jobs, achievements, career aspirations, and current work related activities. Don't forget to list all of those organizations you belong to both on and off the job. Don't include your marital status on the number of children you have. Highlight any awards that you've received and presto—you have all of the ingredients for a competitive résumé.

With the help of that special person, you can produce a power-packed résumé that will take you to the next ladder of your career path.

## Sign Up for a Teleclass

Who ever said you can't learn a new skill on the telephone? One of the hottest new educational products on the marketplace is the teleclass. A teleclass is a one, two, or three-hour workshop all conducted on the telephone. Usually up to 30 people are on the call at the same time, and the session is hosted by a trainer, facilitator, speaker, or coach. The session itself is reasonably priced, with segments varying from highly interactive to highly structured.

Want to become a better speaker? Take a teleclass. Want to learn new tips on balancing work and family? Take a teleclass. Want to learn how to negotiate your next pay raise or promotion? Take a teleclass. Want savvy marketing tips for your business? Take a teleclass.

Teleclasses will expand your horizons in the convenience and comfort of your home or office telephone. I started conducting teleclasses a few years ago, and was amazed at the interest of those who sign up for my sessions. I usually have a cross-section of people across the United States and parts of Canada. Because of the expansiveness of telecommunications, it doesn't matter where you are in order to participate in one of these calls. Tom Antion, a speaker and colleague of mine, actually hosted a teleclass that I participated in that included 600 participants from around the world, all connected by a special telephone bridge line. That was a pretty amazing feat.

Visit my website, **www.TellCarole.com** to learn more about my teleclass programs archived on audio tapes and CDs. If you are a professional speaker or communicator, **www.SpeakerNetNews.com** also offers a variety of teleclasses on many topics in the industry. Professional coaches also use teleclasses for instructional and advisory purposes. You can learn more about their services by visiting the website for the International Coach Federation **www.CoachFederation.org** and the website for Coach University **www.CoachInc.com.**

_____

# *For the culture*

of the teacher to be in the

consciousness of the child,

the culture of the child must

first be in the consciousness

of the teacher.

- Basil Bernstein (1924-2000)

_____

## CHAPTER SIX

# Diversity in a Global World

### Diversity and Empowerment

Diversity is the understanding, management, and appreciation of differences and similarities at the same time. Its very mission speaks to the empowerment each and every one of us must have in order to respect people who are different than we are. It requires us to embrace those individuals who share our values, but not at the expense of those who are different. As simple as the concept is, diversity can be a daunting task if a person or organization is not committed to the cause.

I have taught diversity classes, spoken on diversity, consulted on diversity, and written on diversity issues for nearly 16 years. I've worked with those who were excited about the concept and those who absolutely hated it. And through all of my experiences working with such a wide variety of people I can say that those who are empowered to make a difference usually become strong advocates for diversity.

Diversity and empowerment go hand in hand. Celebrating the spectrum of the human experience requires one to dig deeply into a level of personal integrity that is free of bigotry, hatred, or malice.

Diversity and empowerment demand that trust and respect become an integral part of every meeting, project, relationship, negotiation, or consultation that takes place between two or more people.

Racial and ethnic diversity includes every person on the face of the earth:

| | |
|---|---|
| Blacks | Latino/Latinas |
| African Americans | Pacific Islanders |
| Africans | Asian Americans |
| Whites | Indians |
| Europeans | Arabs |
| South Americans | Middle Easterners |
| Hispanics | South Asians |
| Chicanos | Asians |
| Native Americans / American Indians | Biracial/Bicultural. |

The entire world makes up the diversity spectrum of life.

## The Global Marketplace

In the diversity workshops that I conduct throughout the country, I often test the knowledge of my participants by asking them to tell me how many people live in our world. Since most don't know, they're amazed to find out that at there are over 6.2 billion men, women, and children in our global village. China is the most populous country with nearly two billion people, followed closely by India with more than one billion. And how many people live in the United States you ask? Close to 300 million, only five percent of the world's total population.

Do you have the capacity to wrap your heart, soul, and mind around the world of 6 billion? Or are you like so many, focusing only on the handful of faces that you know in your circle of friends, family and coworkers?

Stretch your mind, expand your horizons, and reach out and touch the faces of people in distant lands unknown.

The best website to acquaint yourself with the current population numbers is the US Census Bureau, **www.census.gov**. That website will give you statistical information on every hamlet in American. On its homepage you'll find a running population clock, updated daily that will help you keep track of total population numbers for the country and the world.

## Get the Census Facts

To find out the latest U.S. and world population numbers, log on to the U.S. Census Bureau website at **www.census.gov**. A few minutes on this site will educate you about the latest statistical analysis compiled from the 2000 census. You can find national data and statistical information for your own hometown.

I encourage you to visit **www.census.gov**. I am constantly amazed at how uninformed people are about the number of human beings who live on the planet and what is the total population of the United States. You can find out what those numbers are, and much more, on the census website. All free of charge, just waiting for you twenty-four hours a day, seven days a week.

Create a census game with your family, friends, and colleagues, and offer a prize to the first person who correctly tells you how many people live in this world. Empower yourself with knowledge, visit **www. census.gov** and share your new found wisdom wherever you go!

## Become a Citizen of the World

*"For the culture of the teacher to be in the consciousness of the child, the culture of the child must first be in the consciousness of the teacher."*

Renowned British sociologist Basil Bernstein's philosophical words are applicable to each one of us. Bernstsein (1924-2000) spent a lifetime teaching and studying the impact of social class, education, and culture on our society. How can we ever expect to live in a truly multicultural world if we don't spend the extra time learning about the extraordinary cultures in our own backyard?

I live in New England, which has become home to a world-wide collection of all types of people; Black, White, Asian, Latino, Native American, Arab American. More than 80% of the students of the Boston Public School system are non-white. In suburban communities in New England and throughout the country ethnic diversity is changing the face of neighborhoods large and small. With these sweeping demographic changes, what are you doing to learn about the backgrounds of your neighbors, co-workers or friends?

*What can we do?* One easy way to expand your diversity experience is to simply strike up a conversation and *ASK* the type of questions that will open up a line of cultural dialogue between you and other people. You'll be amazed at what you find out and how this new knowledge will help you become a citizen of the world.

## Learn About the World

With over 6 billion people on the planet, how can you possibly begin to understand the different cultures around the globe? I know, you're saying to yourself, I barely know the ins and outs out my own community, much less what's going on a continent away.

You can start by ordering Culturegrams from Brigham Young University in Utah at **www.CultureGrams.com**. Over 177 countries are included in the Culturegram series, and they provide the history and respective traditions of each country that they represent. Next visit **www.cia.gov/cia/publications/factbook**. This website is maintained by the Central Intelligence Agency of the US government and includes economic, social, and political profiles of most countries of the world. Stop into your favorite bookstore or office superstore and pick up a copy of Rand McNally's World Facts and Maps (**www.amazon.com**). Search the Internet on your own and discover the customs of the Congo or the luxuries of Liechtenstein.

It's a big world out there and it's waiting for you to find creatively different ways to bring its mysteries and magic into your mind, body and soul.

## Learn More About the World

Learning about the world around us with all of its 6 billion people doesn't have to be confined to a geography class. Whether you're 21 or 71, there are ample opportunities for you to discover the fascinating facts about our global village.

May I suggest that you create *a Family Geography Power Hour,* a time when you and your loved ones or friends can get together and learn more about Cuba, Lebanon, Latvia or the Marshall Islands?

Visit the public library, the greatest free facility in America and check out the books, magazines, maps, tapes and videos containing scores of information about our world.

And don't forget about the rich diversity you have in your own region. Talk to your neighbors from Jamaica, your co-workers from Ireland, or your grocer from Kenya and *ask* them about their native land. It's amazing what they'll share with you if your curiosity will only allow you to ask the right questions.

## Ten-Minute Time-Out

I was amazed and overwhelmed to hear of the tiny infant born to a courageous mother in the trees during a horrific rainstorm in Mozambique. As the rains came down, killing hundreds, destroying homes and flooding the landscape with an ocean of unwanted water, a child was determined to be born in the very tree that sheltered its Mother who used it as a birthing center.

Life is pretty amazing, and survival stories like this one should cause you to shop and focus on the daily circumstances that test the willpower of humanity. I encourage you to think about those battling AIDS in Sub-Saharan Africa. Pray for those fighting famine in countries where jobs are scare and food is hard to find. Reflect on those uttering prayers of protection as religious disagreements lead to unchecked violence in Northern Ireland, Palestine, and Israel.

So the next time you're fussing about not having a new outfit to wear to the dance of the season, just remember how powerful it is to put your own issues on the back burner while you concentrate on mentally reaching out to others in distant lands.

## The World Speaks in Different Tongues

Shout out loud and tell me how many languages and dialects are spoken in the world today. One hundred or 1000? Guess again, because there are a staggering 6,703 languages and dialects spoken in the world today. Don't believe me? Go to **www.sil.org/ethnologue** and count them for yourself.

Over 2100 languages and dialects are spoken in Asia alone. Over 2000 in Africa. The Pacific region counts over 1300 languages and dialects, and the Americas 1000. Europe has the fewest with 225.

In Laos, 5 million people speak 236 languages and dialects. In Nigeria over 300 are spoken. All Chinese throughout the world use one Chinese written language. However, they use more than one *spoken* language. Approximately 70% of Chinese speak Mandarin. More people speak Mandarin than any other language on the planet.

So the next time someone complains to you about people not speaking English, educate them about the varieties of voices spoken from continent to continent.

## World Religions

Close to 85% of North Americans identify themselves as Christians. There are 1200 formal Christian organizations in North America and literally hundreds of religious sects, denominations and cults worldwide, with 12 established major world religions groups boasting over three million followers in each group.

# PERSONAL EMPOWERMENT

The top 12 group of believers/non-believers (those who are faith-based or otherwise) are as follows:

| | |
|---|---|
| 1. Christianity | 2 Billion |
| 2. Islam | 1.2 Billion |
| 3. Hinduism | 786 Million |
| 4. Buddhism | 362 Million |
| 5. Atheism | 211 Million |
| 6. Chinese Folk Religions | 188 Million |
| 7. New Asian Religions | 106 Million |
| 8. Tribal Religions | 91 Million |
| 9. Vodun (Voodoo) | 60 Million |
| 10. Taoism/Other | 20 Million |
| 11. Judaism | 18 Million |
| 12. Sikhism | 16 Million |

There are more than two billion Christians worldwide followed by 1.2 billion who are Islamic. Judiasm is practiced by 18 million people.

Religious, ethical, and non-religious groups continue to form throughout the world, making this topic very difficult to even discuss. To find out more factual information about how the world worships, go to **www.ReligiousTolerance.org**, where you'll find an unbiased representation of world religion, practices and perspectives. I have used this site for several years. The Ontario (Canada) Consultants on Religious Tolerance maintain it.

## Affirmative Action Versus Diversity

Make sure you understand the facts when you argue for or against affirmative action. Created in 1961 by Executive Order 10925, affirmative action takes positive steps to recruit, hire, train, and promote individuals from groups that have traditionally been discriminated against, namely, African Americans, Hispanics, Asians, and white women. Veterans have also benefited from affirmative action.

Affirmative action seeks out *qualified* diverse candidates for employment and educational opportunities and provides a path of upward career mobility based on individual skill sets and performance potential.

Diversity is the practice of understanding, appreciating and ultimately valuing differences and similarities both on and off the job. It's largely a voluntary process and involves all races including white people.

The origins of diversity are deeply embedded in the principles of affirmative action, even though both concepts stand alone in the workplace.

Understand it. Practice it. Spread The Word. Affirmative Action and Diversity are key ingredients for success at home, at school and on the job.

*This hectic world*

forces us to rely

on a cooperative,

unselfish, family structure

to make it all work.

# CHAPTER SEVEN

# *Family Matters*

## Motown Moments

On Easter weekend, 2003, I returned to Detroit, my hometown. It was now five years since my mother's death. My brother wanted me to come home for the holidays, and I was eager to go. My daughters traveled in from Chicago and Hartford, however my niece, Lauren, couldn't attend since her graduation from Pratt Institute was a few short weeks away. She would be receiving her master's degree in interior design on a very special Saturday in May, once again making Wilson and Debbie very proud parents.

Sadness overwhelmed me as soon as I stepped off the airplane. My mother, my anchor, was gone. The city had changed. I felt adrift in a sea of transition.

As luck would have it, I attended a concert by the Funk Brothers, the original studio musicians for Motown Records. Now well into their sixties, these artists are quintessential music masters. They have received two Grammy awards for the soundtrack of their acclaimed documentary film, *Standing in the Shadows of Motown*. These wonderful musicians revived my spirit with every song they belted out that night.

Four black musicians and two white. Still alive. Still pumping out the Motown sound. That evening thousands of black and white fans cheered and danced in their seats. We cheered for the visionary Allan

"Dr. Licks" Slutsky who brought to life to the documentary project that finally recognized these men who were in the shadows of Marvin Gaye, Diana Ross and the Supremes, The Temptations, and the Four Tops.

Little did I realize that the concert would afford me an opportunity to snap their pictures while I waited in line for autographs from Joe Messina, Joe Hunter, Uriel Jones, Bob Babbitt and Jack "Black Jack" Ashford.

They had taken away my sorrow with the songs such as *"Ain't Too Proud To Beg."* For three hours I returned to the rhythms and melodies of my youth—the basement house parties of my teenage years.

*"What's Become of the Broken Hearted." "Cool Jerk." "Shotgun." "My Girl." "I Heard It Through the Grapevine." "Ain't No Mountain High Enough."*

The music filled my soul and reassured me that my loved ones were still with me in spirit. The sounds reminded me that empowerment allows us to grieve, to remember, to embrace, and to connect. The music restored my quest to go deeper into my life journey.

It is in that spirit that I ask you to examine your family connections. Embrace your past while celebrating your family's future. Discover the music buried deeply inside of you as you orchestrate the next move in your life.

## Linking to My Past - Leading the Future

My hero and best friend was my mother, Gwendolyn Juanita Charleston Copeland. Through thick or thin she always stood by my side and watched her youngest offspring find her place in the world. Near the end of her life she said, "Carole, you have finally found your niche." In the final weeks of her robust life in April, 1998, in her hospital room, with monitors and intravenous feeding tubes wrapped encircling her body, she lovingly declared to me, "I adore you." Those words remain in my soul forever. Throughout her life, mother was adored by her family and surrounded by love and affection.

My only brother, Wilson Albert Copeland, II, has a solid reputation as a Detroit trial lawyer. His professional accomplishments earned him admission into the prestigious International Academy of Trial Lawyers. His work with area hospitals ensured that mother was receiving the best care possible in spite of her deteriorating health. His wife, Deborah Fitzgerald Copeland, was ever the nurturing daughter-in-law, and had treated my mother like her very own for decades. Deborah was now juggling hospital visits with the increasing need to care for her own elegant and elderly mother. Their daughter, Lauren, was my favorite niece, and did her best to show concern while continuing her studies at Spelman College.

It was a particularly difficult time for my own daughters. The 1997 death of their brother Mikey was still fresh in their minds, Lorna and Michelle struggled with keeping focused on school and family matters. Lorna was just weeks away from graduating from Spelman. She had just been initiated as a member of Delta Sigma Theta Sorority, the sorority of her grandmother Copeland, her mother and her Aunt Deborah. Michelle was suffering a deeper grief as a freshman at Tuskegee University. Her life would never be the same with her twin brother dead and her grandmother so very ill.

Our mother died on May 5, 1998 in the early hours of that Tuesday morning. The girls were away at school. My brother and sister-in-law at home in Detroit were just waiting for the phone to ring. I was speaking in Salt Lake City, Utah when I received the mournful phone call that my mother was gone. I looked out my hotel window at the mountains, and knew that once again my life had changed forever. In eleven months I had lost my son and now my mother.

It was the end of an era. My father, Wilson Albert Copeland, had died in 1991. A few months later my marriage of 20 years ended. In 1997 Mikey died in a car accident, and now my mother.

We buried my mother the day before Mother's Day. That holiday is now very hard for me to endure. The next weekend my daughter, Lorna, graduated from Spelman. I was overcome with both joy and sadness.

In 1999, my maternal great uncle, Dr. Samuel Prince Charleston, died at 95. He had been a pillar of Columbus, Georgia's African American community. My paternal aunt, Marguerite Copeland of Bel Air, Maryland is now my oldest family member.

Our family has shifted into a new arrangement with new leaders. Now the family mantle rests squarely on the shoulders of my brother and me. We carry on the family legacy now that our parents are gone. Our generation is now in charge and bears the awesome responsibility of honoring our parents through our actions and our commitment to others.

We are the direct links to our ancestors. We represent the present. We shape the lives of our offspring. They are the future. We possess the family stories that will strengthen our children to do well in the present and to keep moving to high ground. In our remaining years we will be charged with ensuring that our family legacy lives on from our generation to the next. Whatever our elders have taught us that is good, we must pass on to others, so that the best in our culture will continue.

## Finding the Balance Between Work and Family

"The key for us to each remember, is that we are a team." That's the secret technique that gets Howard Amidon through the balancing act he and his spouse endure as busy working parents. At one time they both commuted an hour each way to work while racing back to beat the 6 p.m. daycare deadline.

Angeline Scott says her husband is the key ingredient for their family's success, and "she'd go nuts without him."

This hectic world forces us to rely on a cooperative, unselfish family structure to make it all work. It's refreshing to know that couples are functioning as a team to make their households hum.

Spouses create family goals together. Work with your spouse or significant other to create a healthy home environment that will bring you closer together in mind, body, and soul.

## Family Rituals

What kind of rituals can you establish in your family unit? Is there a way that you can tie in an important family ritual to help bring you closer together?

Take the advice of busy single mom, doctoral student and Boston Alumnae President of Delta Sigma Theta, Natalie Carithers and eat at least one meal together. Before her children left for college Natalie insisted on eating breakfast or dinner with her son and daughter, and she used the time to listen to them, and to teach etiquette techniques and conversational skills to her young adults.

While I was growing up in Detroit, I was expected to learn one new Bible verse each Sunday and recite it at the breakfast table. With that ritual, my family helped to strengthen the spiritual side of my life while they provided my grits, biscuits and sausage every weekend.

Figure out a way that you can start a family ritual that will anchor the connection you cherish to those important people in your life.

## Rituals for Singles

Who says you have to have children and a spouse to start a personal ritual? Yes, you can begin a ritual of your very own as a single person while navigating the ins and outs of your busy life. Why not select a special time each week or two that's dedicated to rejuvenating your sprit and zest for living? Set aside a pamper day for yourself at home, spa, gym, or athletic field. And yes, men it's o.k. for you to include a solo bubble bath as part of your ritual, too.

If you choose to include other people in your ritual, reach out to friends, family, and folks who appreciate your company. Prepare a meal, pick a theme, and have a hot lively discussion over delicious food. Think of a time when you can dine with that special young person who looks up to you in admiration.

Enjoy your life as an empowered single person. You deserve new ways to reach out and embrace the joys of living.

## Family Night In - Part 1

It wasn't that long ago when families gathered around the fireplace, kitchen table, or other warm spot in the house to tell stories of triumph, struggle and new possibilities. Before television, the Internet, or cell phones, families would entertain each other without the need of electronic contraptions that often prevent the gift of direct contact with one another.

Pick an evening once a month and declare the time as *Family Night In*. Pick a topic and create discussion questions the will engage your family in a good old-fashioned debate for hours. Or find an arts and crafts project that will require every member of your family to complete.

It's amazing what you will discover about your sister, brother, parent or child just by turning off the television and letting the vocal chords flow. *Family Night In* can empower you to reach out and touch your loved ones in a special new way.

## Family Night In - Part 2

*Family Night In* can become a wonderful way to provide free entertainment for your own family without turning on the television or leaving your front door. You can really become a homegrown hero by letting your children design a special evening of good family fun.

Here's how to start. Announce to your kids that a designated evening next month is being set aside for them to plan. Let them know that they are responsible for creating a special evening of fun, conversation, and entertainment. Support them by checking in to see how their planning process is taking shape.

They can't rent videos, turn on the television, play their CDs or DVDs. However, the children can use their imagination to put together the best evening your family has had in years. Singing, dancing or acting in a live performance should garner special recognition.

*Family Night In* allows your children to plan an evening of fun-filled activities for the whole family. They'll surprise you with how much talent they can pack into a single night of festivities.

# PERSONAL EMPOWERMENT

## Family Reunion Reporter

Can't wait to pack your bags and fly off to your family reunion? Here's what I want you to do: take us along for the ride. I know you can't fit all of us in your suitcase, but I do want you to pack your tape recorder, camera, pad, pencil and video camera along for the journey.

Capture as much as you can on film, disc, tape and on paper. Reflect on those old stories that relatives tell. Think about how valuable they will be for your colleagues who need to learn about your culture directly from you.

There's enough bad news in the newspaper about gang bangers and inner city poverty. Now is your chance to counter the negativity by reporting about your family's rich heritage when you get back to the job.

Become an on the scene reunion reporter and start telling your co-workers about your black, white, Latino, Asian, Arab, or Indian family who's making a significant difference in our society.

## Family Reunion Reflection - Part 1

A wave of pride filled my heart when I recently attended my family reunion. Held in Baltimore, Maryland and hosted by the Lansey arm of the Gaines family, I become acutely aware of just how connected our family has been to American history. In 1933 a young Thurgood Marshall defended and won a civil rights case involving my cousin, Donald Gaines Murray, who was denied admission to the University of Maryland Law School. Our family owned institution, Ideal Federal Savings Bank, has been in operation in Baltimore since 1932. Every family connects to history in ways that can encourage family members if they learn their family stories.

There are golden nuggets in your family tree, but you must stop long enough to find them. Start your own family reunion if you don't have one, or enhance the one you have by finding your family connections to American history.

## Family Reunion Reflection - Part 2

Attending several of my family reunions have connected me with my relatives in a very special way. Our roots stretch back to the plantations of Georgia dating back to the late 1700s, but our branches cover the entire United States. Cousin Clarence Gaines of Chicago has spent countless hours meticulously researching our family tree for more than eight years. It makes me proud to know that my family includes two Bishops of the African Methodist Episcopal Church, bankers, lawyers, teachers, government professionals, entrepreneurs, cooks, domestics, and truck drivers.

Start your own family reunion by getting your relatives together for a one-day event sometime in the next two years. Your reunion can be held every other year, and it doesn't have to be fancy. A family picnic or potluck dinner will provide the right atmosphere for coming together on common ground. Start by writing down everything you know about your family and use the Internet to search for more clues into your past.

Family reunions equal family empowerment.

Start your tradition today.

## Start Your Own Family Reunion

I understand. You're a bit jealous when you hear your friends talk about their upcoming family reunion that's taking place *down home* in a few weeks. You don't want to attend theirs; you just want your family to create one of your own. Why don't *you* become that bold and courageous family member and get it started in the coming year?

Make your phone calls and start this project on a small-scale basis. Try to have a one-day event at a local park, beach, or a convenient destination where the family can meet. Keep it simple, and use it as a launching pad for future events. If you don't want to do all the work yourself, delegate tasks to other family members who can help with the big day of activities.

Pack your camera, your tape recorder, your video camera and your pad and pencil and get ready for the inauguration of your family reunion that will start you on a new path of inner cultural connection.

## Yes, African Americans Can Build a Family Tree

*Black Genealogy* by Charles L. Blockson is one of a number of books on the market to help African Americans trace their roots back to Mother Africa. One of several books available to conduct this type of research, it provides much need background information to understand how slaves were accounted for on the plantations of the Americas.

The next time you are traveling to your hometown, take along your tape recorder, video camera, pad and pencil and capture every single story that Aunt Esther tells you on her front porch. Also during your next family reunion, let each member complete your family tree to the best of their ability. Collect all of the information they share with you, use *Black Genealogy* as a reference, do an Internet search and discover new facts about your family's rich history. Then start a family newsletter so you can continue searching throughout the year.

## Social Etiquette - Kids' Style

If I'm stepping on toes, I'm doing it in the spirit of love and good intentions. Our kids need help in social etiquette, manners, and grace. I am around young people enough to know that so often what they perfect on computers, in the classroom, and on the dance floor they're woefully lacking in table manners, social skills, and interactive style. Because we're an "eat on the go" society, many of our young people would be clueless if they ever attended a formal dinner. They wouldn't know which fork to use first. Worse, so often when they receive lovely gifts purchased with someone's hard-earned time and money, the last thing on their mind is sending out a thank-you note of appreciation. We are the generation who must teach the next generation to be considerate!

So, parents, grandparents, single relatives, and friends listen up. Our jobs are not yet complete in teaching young people social etiquette skills. Let's get busy learning those skills ourselves before we pass them on. Our kids will thank us for the knowledge we share with them.

## Real Men - Real Fathers

The doom and gloom about fathers in our communities overshadows the influence of many men who are doing their jobs and making a difference for their families in our society. To those who stand tall as family men of action, we salute you.

You know who you are and that your love, devotion and dedication set you apart in a world where so often men who misbehave are mistakenly profiled as the poster boys for our society. We appreciate your dedication as we ask you to teach it to others. Please pass it on.

---

# *I learned as a parent*

I could not teach our sons all of life's lessons, because I didn't know many of them myself.

- Maurice B. Wright

---

In his chapter in *Brothers Together*, a wonderful anthology edited by Joe Gould, Maurice B. Wright, Boston community leader, husband, and dedicated father of twins states, "I learned that as a parent, I could not teach our sons all of life's lessons, because I didn't know many of them myself." He credits extended family members as the secret ingredient in creating "a rich environment in which children can thrive."

It does take a village to raise a child, and fathers who are making a difference in the lives of children everywhere deserve high praise for their courage, commitment, and dedication to serve as real men and real fathers.

## Make Your Own Family History

Each February during Black History Month we pay tribute to the contributions of men and women who have made a difference in the African American tradition. While their achievements are notable, let's not forget the reality that Black History can be made every single day when you empower yourself to go the distance and break records of your own.

Perhaps you could become the first in your family to start a read-a-thon with neighborhood kids in your community. Be bold and outrageous and start a letter-writing campaign to media and entertainment executives pointing out the many ways that they can increase diversity on television, in movies, and on the radio. Strike out on your own by becoming the best civic activist your neighborhood has ever seen.

Break records, make a difference, and create new ways to celebrate Black History with you in mind.

*Reach your dreams*

by putting yourself

on a self-talk diet.

# CHAPTER EIGHT

# *Self Care*

## Self-Control and Attitude Adjustment

Your attitudes, mood swings, and emotions, including anger, sorrow and fear all churn away in your mind just waiting to pop up at a moment's notice when called into action. You hold the key to what comes rushing forth when your boss hits your hot button, or your spouse sends you into orbit when your bank account is overdrawn.

The older I grow, the more I realize that life is a combination of circumstances that we do control and events that we do not control. We do control our attitude and how we react to the situations that come our way. It's a matter of using self-control and learning how to manage the emotional hot buttons of our existence.

One of the best ways to begin working on your self control is to learn how to expect the unexpected. Let's face it. Nothing in life is guaranteed, except death and taxes. Since problems will occur, get ready for them in advance by preparing yourself financially, physically and mentally. People will get angry and may get mad at you from time to time. When the anger hits, control your emotions by not flying off the handle.

Finding self-control isn't half as challenging as maintaining self-control. By maintaining your self-control, you will be better equipped to keep pace with your emotional tempo while adjusting your attitude when your problems begin to find your weak spots.

*Self-Control.* Find it. Keep it.

*Attitude Adjustment.* Reinforce it.

Take control of your life by taking control of yourself.

## Go On a Self-Talk Diet

Reach your dreams by putting yourself on a self-talk diet. Build a list of positive affirmations that are so uplifting that you will tell yourself over and over again about the many ways that you will reach your dreams.

Use expressions like these to build up your positive affirmation zone:

> With faith, prayer, and action, I can achieve.

> I have what it takes to overcome my obstacles and reach my goals.

> I have the patience, the persistence, and the potential to make it happen.

> I have come through the storms of my past. I know that I can handle any setback that comes my way!

Your personal self-talk diet limits you to these type of positive reinforcers. Doubt, disbelief, and self-sabotage are strictly prohibited from your self-talk diet.

Talk to yourself, believe in yourself, and make your new self-talk diet work for you.

## Positive Self-Talk

When was the last time you told yourself, "I love you?" Have you complimented yourself on how gifted you are? And did you pat yourself on the back for solving that tough problem all by yourself?

Without being narcissistic, you'd be amazed at how powerful self-talk can be. Positive self-talk can wake you up to the opportunities of a new morning. Self-talk can put you to bed with the accomplishments of your day's activities. It's easy to slip into the habit of being particularly tough on yourself, zeroing in on that unwanted pimple or concentrating on the extra pounds that don't want to melt away.

It takes extra effort to minimize our self-criticism by doubling the amount of time we use to celebrate what makes us so special.

So pick up that mirror, look at that important face in the glass, and tell yourself how special you are to yourself, to your family, and to the community at large.

## Take Time to Think

Called the father of modern philosophy, René Descartes was a 17th century thinker, mathematician and scientist. In 1620, Descartes came up with his most famous statement: "I think, therefore I am." This thought occurred to him as he warmed himself by a stove while serving in the military in Germany.

When was the last time you took time out of your busy schedule, found a relaxing comfortable spot and just explored your thoughts? Maybe it's a solo walk on the beach, or sitting in a darkened room in your house, or finding the right spot outdoors with the birds chirping away in the trees.

Taking time out to think is one of the most powerful ways to fortify your attitude and emotional well being for all of those daily obstacles and problems just waiting to visit your life. Prepare for them by setting aside a few moments here and there for a one on one thinking session with yourself.

## Treat Yourself to a Taste of Luxury

The health and fitness business is a booming multi-billion dollar industry. There are many ways that you can cap off your fitness and health care routine by treating yourself to a full body massage and pampering session. I've indulged in many massages, my favorite one at the Doral Golf Resort and Spa in Miami, Florida. Their spa is housed in a massive three story building right on their resort property. I still savor the experience of visiting there after a business conference that was held at the resort. I stayed on an extra day to enjoy an eight-hour spa treatment of hydrotherapy, a healthy lunch, and one of the best one-hour massages I've ever had.

Quite often there's no time to pack a bag and leave town to pamper your spirit. In cities and towns throughout the globe there are large and small spas to fit your needs and your wallet. Why not find a locally trained licensed muscular therapist to rub away the stress and tension from a hard day's work?

There are all sorts of massages these days, including the traditional Swedish, shiatsu, therapeutic, aromatherapy, and reflexology. Check the Internet where you will find dozens of sites that will help you navigate the spa industry by finding the right treatment for you.

A full body massage will leave you relaxed, less tense, and ready to conquer the world. It's the perfect way to complete your fitness routine by helping prepare you for the rigors of you work and family activities.

## Head Gear

Looking like Tina Turner on my 50th birthday seemed like just a dream until I buckled down and got to work on making it happen. A few years ago I joined Weight Watchers and a fitness center and visualize myself singing Proud Mary live on stage in a few short years.

But mere exercise and pumping iron is only the beginning of creating an empowered lifestyle. You've got to mentally and emotionally embrace the new *you* before you even get started. You must do your *head work* so that when you're ready to throw in the towel, your inner voice will tell you to *keep going*.

Check your head, tell yourself that you're a winner, and get ready to reap the rewards as your game plan moves forward.

## Inside Out Healthy Living

Getting in shape won't be enough if you don't spend some time grooming your MIND for a more empowered way of life. Ever met a dashingly handsome gentleman or a drop dead gorgeous woman whose physical attractiveness was alluring, but there was something missing in the attitude department?

While you're watching your calories and gearing up for that five mile jog around the neighborhood, don't forget about feeding your mind with positive self-talk and filling your head with useful information that will take you to the next level in life. Find a few minutes three or four times a week where you can just be alone with your own thoughts. If you're a busy parent or live in a congested household, you might find your quiet time locked in the bathroom while you're dressing in the morning.

Feeding your mind with a fresh dose of encouragement, energy and enthusiasm will do wonders for your personal growth. Go ahead and shape up that body, but don't forget about fortifying you mental state of being.

## Keep the Weight Off

You and I need to be reminded to stay fit and healthy for the rest of the year. It's so easy to put back on the weight you worked hard to lose if you're not careful about keeping your fitness regiment on schedule. I attend many conferences and banquets and know just how easy it is to pick up an extra piece of bread or scoop up that delicious serving of chocolate mousse.

So get back to work and take off those extra pounds. Instead of taking the elevator up to the second floor take the stairs. When the hunger pains hit at 3 p.m. pick up some carrots instead of cheese and crackers. And tell yourself that you can keep that weight off because you deserve to look good for your family, friends, and yourself. Feel good, look good, and work on being healthy.

## Attitude and Fitness

At 49 years young, I'm sure not what I used to be. My clothes fit in strange new ways, and there seems to be a new gray hair, wrinkle, and bulge of fat creeping up on me every single week. I look at my youthful daughters at 23 and 27 years old, and see a reflection of myself from years gone by. Age has definitely become a reality in my life.

Yet, I still hold on to my secret goal of entering the Tina Turner lookalike contest on my 50$^{th}$ birthday. I know that regular exercise, a balanced diet, and a positive outlook is the only way that I'm gonna get there. You see, before you can shed those pounds and sign up for that extended warranty on your life, you must first prepare your mind for a new attitude about your personal fitness routine.

My goal is to give Tina Turner a run for her money is at hand for me. It keeps me focused on how important my diet and fitness routines are in my life. Figure out your fitness goal, adjust your attitude, and get ready to live the good life through a results-driven fitness plan designed just for you.

## Walk for Your Health

You can do it! It's not too late for you to start your fitness plan by adding a walking strategy. C'mon, stop making excuses and figure out which three days for the next three weeks you're going to take that walk around your downtown streets, your local lake or pond, the beach, or just around the neighborhood.

You can do it, so stop talking yourself out of it. It's amazing how trim you will become by just adding a brisk half hour walk to your daily activities every other day or so.

Pick your route, get on those sneakers, and don't forget to stretch beforehand, put on that upbeat music, and walk for your mind, body and spirit.

# PERSONAL EMPOWERMENT

## The Healthy You

Blue Cross Blue Shield of Massachusetts has an effective Six-Point plan to keep you healthy and nutritionally fit.

*Step One:* Eat a variety of nutrient-rich foods, such as bread, whole grain products, fruits, vegetables, dairy products, meats, poultry and fish.

*Step Two:* Choose most of what you eat from plant sources and make meat a side dish.

*Step Three:* Eat five or more servings of fruits and vegetables each day.

*Step Four:* Eat six or more servings of bread, pasta, and grains each day.

*Step Five:* Eat fewer high-fat foods, especially those from animal sources...which include saturated fats from meat, poultry and high-fat dairy products.

*Step Six:* Keep your intake of simple sugars to a minimum.

Follow this six-step plan, and you'll extend your life and quality of life well into the future.

## Focus on Fiber

One of the best ways to improve your nutrition is to include plenty of fiber in your diet. The recommended daily allotment for fiber is 20 to 35 grams even though the average person consumes only 10 grams a day. Fiber can lower your serum cholesterol levels, and a diet rich in fiber can decrease your risk of diverticular disease.

Fiber can be found in certain breakfast cereals or oatmeal, raw fruits, vegetables, wheat bread, beans and even popcorn. Fiber is an excellent source of regulating your body and that's good news for maintaining a healthy lifestyle.

So get on a three day a week exercise plan, make sure that fiber is a part of your food routine, and energize yourself for a better tomorrow.

## Creating a Food Journal

Psssssst. This is Carole. Your health police officer just making sure that you're paying attention to all of that food you're stuffing in your mouth every day. You set a goal for yourself to drop a few pounds, but you haven't even begun to put your plan into action yet. So… I'm issuing you a warning ticket to get on track before another day goes by.

Start by writing down everything that you eat in a spiral bound notebook. Tedious eh? And you're already saying, "I don't have the time to do that!" If I can do it—and I have for the past two years—I know you can do it. You'll be amazed what goes down your throat and how much you pack into that expanding stomach of yours. Write down everything you eat and figure out what needs to stay on your food list and what needs to get tossed.

Start that healthy eating pattern right now and watch your waistline shrink and your energy level ramp up.

It's a discipline that makes you stop and think about what you put in your mouth. I learned how to do it at Weight Watchers almost two years ago and I'm still doing it every single day. It's one of those magic bullets that will help you keep the weight off.

What's the secret? Simple. Keep a food journal of everything you eat. It may sound draconian but believe me it really works.

At the beginning of your day or at the very end write down the foods you ate for breakfast, lunch, and dinner. Don't cheat just write it all down. And don't forget those mid-meal snacks, too. Count up your calories or points and you'll figure out the pattern of your eating habits. Once you know your pattern you'll be able to anticipate your hunger pangs BEFORE you open up that big bag of sour cream chips.

Know your body, know your food habits, and control the way you keep yourself fit and trim.

## African American Food Watch

Third cup of regular coffee, eh? Are you making a steady diet of fried chicken, french fries and a double dip chocolate sundae?

Well, it's wake up time for the African American community, because a steady diet of grease, fatback and mounds of butter will put you in the coronary unit of your local hospital quicker than you can imagine. It's time to take a serious look at what you eat each day and rethink your food intake.

You can actually learn to love salads with balsamic vinaigrette dressing, grilled fish or chicken and lots of fresh fruits with your new positive approach to diet and fitness. Plan to start each day with a healthy breakfast including oatmeal, lowfat yogurt and decaffeinated coffee or tea. And don't forget the most powerful drink on the planet, water. Drinking up to three liters of water every day will do wonders for your kidneys and internal organs.

So you decide. You can grease your way to the graveyard, or pick the extended warranty plan for life by eating healthy vittles and drinking lots of water.

## Healthy Snacks

You can learn to enjoy raw carrots as a healthy snack instead of that big bag of potato chips you wolf down at work every afternoon at 3 p.m. Now that you're at least thinking of the right fitness routine and workable food plan for a more shapely YOU, don' t forget about those mid-meal cravings you sometimes get that drive you to corner store for high calorie snacks. The next time you get the urge, make a detour to your local grocery store and stock up on raw vegetables like carrots, celery, or broccoli.

You should even try something new like rice cakes that are low in calories, or trail mix (with sunflower seeds and raisins) that will give you the energy without the high calories of chips or candy bars.

Now I'm not saying you have to ban all sweet stuff forever! Just try out a carrot, celery stalk, or rice cake for the next week or two and see if you can acquire a taste for the healthy stuff.

Continue to exercise, change your snack menu, drink plenty of water, and pat yourself on the back for trimming down to a new wonderful you!

*You have what it takes*

to become a self starter.

Only you can make

the important contributions

on your job and in your family

that demonstrate your skills.

# CHAPTER NINE

# *Take Action*

Now that you have explored the full spectrum of life, let's review some action-packed ways to initiate your empowerment plan consistently and effectively both on and off your job.

With dedication, focus, and a commitment to life an empowered live, get ready for all of the new opportunities that will come as a direct result of your efforts.

It's all up to you. You have what it takes to become a self starter. Only you and make the important contributions on your job and in your family that demonstrate your skills.

## Think, Plan, Act

Want to take control of the success factors in your life? Spend a few moments this week visualizing your milestones for the year. Close your eyes and think about how this year will take shape and when you want the milestones to happen. If your car is begging for replacement, start formulating plans on how and when you're going to replace it. If repair work on your home won't wait another year, break down this daunting task and determine how and when they will take place.

Achieving goals has everything to do with planning. Determining how and when to achieve them will take a bite out of procrastination, panic, and unforeseen obstacles.

## Your Balancing Quotient

The demands of life are making it tougher for most of us to balance work and family responsibilities. But my friend and colleague, Certified Speaking Professional Judy Buch, said it best: "Balance is not a scales concept, but a teeter-totter concept." She also admitted that her hand was never raised for the "Ms. Balance of the Year" either.

What's the right balance for your life? How can you prioritize your work and family activities to maximize the most out of each week without keeling over in exhaustion? When will you learn how to delegate and offload those tasks that should really be handled by the people around you? Isn't it time to take off your superwoman or superman suit and find new ways to get things done both on and off your job?

Figure out your balance quotient and you'll add years to your life. Prioritize what's important and share the rest with staff, colleagues, family and friends.

## Your 21 Day Empowerment Plan - Part 1

Cigarette smoking is habit-forming. And taking too many pain killers can become habit-forming. But did you realize that you have the ability to make empowerment habit-forming as you strengthen and fortify the balance in your life?

Your empowerment process will kick in after 21 days of repeated activity and self-discipline. Just think, in three short weeks you can open up the possibilities that await your future. The discipline of positive self-talk will take root, and fortify your inner spirit to finish that degree, tackle that tough project, or face those family challenges that desperately need attention.

Just 21 days. Three weeks. And you will discover that empowerment indeed resides within your inner spirit. Habit forming, energy-boosting empowerment is your ticket to the dreams of your success.

## Your 21 Day Empowerment Plan - Part 2

Creating a 21 day habit-forming empowerment plan will not shield you from problems, setbacks, disappointments, or doubts. Those are the everyday realities of life. What a 21-day empowerment plan will do is prepare you for the obstacles that are bound to come your way.

It's important to expect obstacles to come into your life by preparing for them in advance. Start off each day with a morning ritual of prayer, meditation, journaling, and/or regular exercise. Go through each day's activities so you know what's ahead of you. Focus on your life goals and know that your empowered spirit will handle any crisis or setback.

By expecting the unexpected, you'll be ready to face the troubles of this world with a calm, prepared plan of attack. Habit-forming empowerment will get you ready for any roller coaster ride that life throws your way.

## Your 21 Day Empowerment Plan - Part 3

Why is a habit-forming empowerment plan so important in tackling problems? Because it gives you the mental toughness to ultimately resolve or discard problems that are bound to come your way.

The daily ritual of mental preparedness will help you properly confront those problems when they sneak up or come tumbling through your doorstep. It's confronting our problems that we often don't want to face. We run and hide and hope that they'll go away. Or we blow up in a rage and assume that our anger will do the talking for us.

Your empowerment plan will allow you to stare your problems in the face, dissect all the complex parts, and ultimately find the solutions needed to resolve the issues.

Habit-forming empowerment is the ultimate roadmap for your journey to a more fulfilling and productive life.

## Habit-Forming Morning Rituals

In three short weeks, you can discover new ways to establish an empowerment plan of action for yourself and your family. Start every day off with a workable, realistic routine. Perhaps it can include a brief meditation, prayer, or moments of silence. Next, go over the action items that must be accomplished for the day. Pull out that journal next to your bedside and capture your inner thoughts on paper. Finally, get in a few sit ups and stretches to get your body in shape for a turbocharged, action-packed day.

I know what you're saying. *"I don't have time for all that! My mornings are too tight for a routine!"* Trust me, by establishing a morning ritual you'll prepare your mind, body, and spirit for the excitement and anxiety that awaits you.

Start the habit-forming-21 day morning ritual that will make empowerment a no-brainer for you. Try it and watch the spring in your step improve each and every day.

## Gaining Financial Independence

I'm constantly trying to learn as much as I can from the experts. A financial expert I trust is Ray Barrows who teaches courses that help the average layperson understand financial jargon and the stock market. Do you know that when you invest your money on a consistent basis that your money will grow in time thanks to the magic of *compound interest?*

Compound interest is the interest earned on previously accumulated interest as well as the principal. The more money you save or invest on a regular basis, the greater your wealth will grow because of the value of compound interest. You won't see your wealth accumulate in the early years of your investment plan; however, after ten years your money will grow like crazy.

No matter how much money you sock away each month, your money will work for you when you create a longterm investment plan of action for your life. From $25 to $2500 a month, you can create wealth by simply saving a specific amount every single month and diligently investing in your future. The power of compound interest will do the rest.

Social Security may not meet all of your needs when you retire. To offset the additional money you will need in your senior years, why not create a financial plan that will guarantee you an income in your golden years?

Find a qualified financial planner to help you, and read newspapers like *Investors Business Daily* and *The Wall Street Journal*. Empower yourself by planning your financial game plan for your future.

## Step By Step Empowerment

Two steps forward. One step backward. Step to the side and step in place. Step to the music. Step in silence.

Don't have a clue about your future? *Keep stepping.*

Disappointed with your relationship? *Keep stepping.*

Children out of control? *Keep stepping.*

Don't know how to balance your home life with work?

*Keep stepping.*

When life hands you a golden nugget, step lightly. When your friends or loved ones cry out in despair, step next to them. When you're feeling all alone, step over to that which comforts you in a wholesome and healthy way. When negativity nags your spirit, flush it from your system.

*Keep stepping. Step on and celebrate your empowerment, your goodness and your strength.*

## Practice Cell Phone Courtesy

The age of technology is simply marvelous, but with it comes new rules on courtesy, behavior and practices that will transform you from being ill-mannered to having a touch of class. In her book *Get Along, Get Ahead: 101 Courtesies For The New Workplace*, motivational speaker and author Karen Hinds spells out new rules for our age of technology. She suggests turning off cell phones and beepers during meetings. Put your phone on a flash or vibrating mode so people won't turn around and stare if your phone rings at the wrong time during that important committee session.

When speaking on a cell or regular phone, lower your voice so people across the street won't hear your conversation. Pick an appropriate time and place to check messages when using your cell phone.

Follow Karen's suggestions and the marvels of your technological toy won't get you labeled as an obnoxious *"phone-a-holic."*

## "Thank You" Power

Never underestimate the power of the written word. Your sentiments will speak volumes when you sit down and hand-write a thank you note showing your appreciation and kindness of another person.

Step ahead of the other candidates and write a thank you note as soon as your job interview has ended. You'd be surprised at how many people never take this important step in the job-hunting quest. Taking the time to thank a potential employer just may give you a career advantage and distinguish you from other candidates.

Did you receive a special gift from a loved one, colleague or friend? Send them a thank you note letting them know just how much you appreciate their thoughtfulness.

What about that strong sales presentation you delivered for that business deal you're after? Send out a note of thanks to your prospective client, and send one to the secretary or administrative assistant, too.

Discover how far reaching your power can spread by simply stating in writing your thankfulness.

## Checkpoint Questions

Schedule time to take stock of where your empowerment journey is taking you by asking yourself the following questions:

1. How motivated are you in continuing your weight loss program?

2. Are you going to the gym or exercising three times a week?

3. Have you cut back on fried foods?

4. Are you drinking more water each day?

5. How successful are you in establishing a solid money management routine?

6. Are you able to pay your bills on time with some money left over?

7. Are you regularly saving money and accumulating wealth?

8. Are you saving for those rainy days ahead?

9. Are you spending quality time with family and friends?

10. Are you taking more time for yourself and your thoughts?

11. Are you stretching to achieve your goals by visualizing your dreams?

12. Do you feel more empowered each day?

Ask yourself these questions and you'll stay on track for the empowerment ride in store for you.

## Let It Go

Your past is history.

*Let it go.*

Didn't make all of your goals last year?

*Let it go.*

Can't seem to put that relationship behind you?

*Let it go.*

Facing disappointments, setbacks and challenges?

*Let them go.*

Do you feel the fear that creeps up every time you face uncertainty?

*Let it go.*

Can you feel that procrastination streak keeping you from reaching your goals take hold?

*Let it go!*

Let go of all the baggage that stands in your way, and fly on the wings of your tomorrow.

*Let It Go.*

## Go Back To School

Is your job giving you the blues? Is a possible layoff or termination an unfortunate possibility? Maybe this is the perfect time to go back to school.

I know what you're thinking. *"I don't have the time, I'm too old, and I don't have two nickels to rub together for any tuition payments."* I am living witness that if you put your mind to it, the time, energy and money will come.

This world is changing so rapidly that it's an imperative for us to sharpen our skills through some level of advanced education. You can go to school part time, full time or on weekends. You can even take classes online. The important thing to remember is to first make the decision to return to school and expect everything thereafter to fall into place.

Returning to school may be an adjustment for you but I know that you can do it. Get that book bag out and educate your mind with some brand new knowledge.

## Managing Chaos

In her book *Indispensable Employees* author and consultant Martha Fields states, "In our ever-changing society and workplace it is important that people do try to bring some type of harmony into their lives by managing chaos and ambiguity." You know that you're on your road to empowerment when can master the juggling act that can either keep you on your toes or turn you into a pillar of salt.

What's the hidden secret in managing the chaos in your life? It's finally getting to the point where you accept the things you can AND cannot control. I've learned that the hard way through the disappointments, disasters, deaths and denials I've dealt with in the last decade of my life. And I've found out that once you find ways to cope with change and uncertainty you can maneuver through the muck and mire of life's triumphs and tribulations.

So fortify your coping skills, learn how to let go, roll with the punches, and let life unfold in a new and refreshingly different way.

## Becoming Approachable

How easy is it for you to take criticism from others? Are you approachable enough to receive feedback from people who only want to help you develop as an empowered individual?

Take stock of how sturdy your pride is and ask yourself the following question, *"Am I big enough to receive constructive criticism from others without becoming defensive and vindictive toward those who have the courage to approach me?"* Be honest and answer the question. If the answer is YES, you're on the right path for continuous personal improvement. If you've honestly answered NO, figure out how you can manage your pride while working on your weak spots.

It's not easy to evaluate your approachability, but I invite you to open the door to those who will give you the feedback you really need to succeed.

## Reading Power

There is no greater resource known to mankind than the power of reading. Through reading you can transform your own ignorance on a subject into an ocean of newfound knowledge. Reading can take you places in the world you never thought existed! Reading can turn your sadness into joy when you select the right book, magazine, newspaper or journal. A ten to fifteen minute reading session each day will do wonders for expanding your mind.

The best thing about reading is that you have options on how you read. You can do it the old fashioned way by cracking open a book and reading each word line by line. Or you can pop an audio cassette or CD in your walkman or stereo system, and listen to the spoken word via a "book on tape." I've listened to countless unabridged books on tape while driving in my car, and find them an extremely valuable entertainment/education source. You can get books on tape at your local library free of charge and listen to Toni Morrison's *The Bluest Eye* or Frank McCourt's *Angela's Ashes*.

Reading is power! Discover its potency every single day. Written word. Spoken word. The choice is yours.

## Your Own Guinness Book of World Records

While hunting with friends, Sir Hugh Beaver wondered which game bird was fastest. No one knew, so Beaver asked London statisticians to compile a book of such records. The result was the *Guinness Book of World Records,* first published in 1955. Today it includes records for feats from dance marathons to pogo-stick jumping.

Ever thought about setting up your own *Guinness Book of World Records?* Why not set up one in your family and celebrate your son or daughter's record on having a clean bedroom? Or what about the number of consecutive weeks you haven't used profanity? Or the number of books you're going to read this season?

Challenge yourself and find new ways that you can document those magic moments with your own personal *Guinness Book of World Records.* Try it and make history with your family, friends and co-workers.

## Start a Family Scrapbook

Why not take all of your family memories, photos, achievements, and treasures and capture them in a family scrapbook? A popular craft activity, scrapbooks are an excellent way to capture the essence of your family experience in one or more volumes of a custom-designed scrapbook.

There are countless instruction manuals on how to start a scrapbook that you can purchase at local arts and crafts stores. Those stores will also carry three ring binders, papers, and all the tools you'll need to begin your project. All you need to supply are pictures, mementos, newspaper clippings, artifacts, and all of the other keepsakes you want to include in your memory book.

You can even participate in National Scrapbook Day. It's a day designated for people throughout the United States, Puerto Rico, Canada, the United Kingdom, Germany, Australia, New Zealand, and Taiwan to gather in homes, meeting rooms and community centers to share memories while working on scrapbook photo albums.

National Scrapbook Day is observed every year and is designed to foster the value of creating and completing photo albums while sharing memories in a fun, social, and quilting-bee type atmosphere.

If you'd like more information about starting your scrapbook or participating in National Scrapbook Day contact Robin Thompson at **speaker@robinthompson.com.**

## Reaching Out to Senior Citizens

Personal empowerment allows us many opportunities to reach out to others by showing that we care. One of the best ways to demonstrate your personal touch is by giving your time and energy to a senior citizen in your family or neighborhood.

Find out ways that you can be of service to them. Is there a senior citizen that you can help? Can you read to them? Help them with their household chores? Go grocery shopping for them? Water their plants? Take them to the drug store or the beauty shop? Perhaps you can arrange with others to provide transportation for them to and from their worship center each week. Maybe you can give them a hand with holiday shopping, or help by picking out that special gift for their family and friends.

Giving your time and energy can bring joy to a senior citizen in the golden years of life. It's what community is all about.

## A Letter to Yourself

One of the most effective workshop activities I have presented to my audiences is *A Letter To Yourself*. At the conclusion of each session I allow participants to write a letter to him/herself stating a single goal that can be achieved in the foreseeable future. The letter is signed, placed in an envelope, sealed, self-addressed, and passed to the facilitator. Each letter is then stored, unopened for six months before being mailed back to the sender.

Teresa Lammey recently proved just how powerful the *Letter to Self* can be. She attended an empowerment workshop for single women I conducted two years ago. In her letter to herself she outlined a plan that included buying a home in the near future. It was merely a dream for Teresa, because money was tight for this single mother of two, and the prospect of becoming a homeowner seemed slim. However, the letter planted a powerful seed in Teresa's mind. Now, two years later, Teresa has met a wonderful man, is engaged, and is making plans with her fiancé, Guy Reid, to purchase a home after they are married. That's what happens when the power of suggestion takes the form of a letter and keeps you accountable for your actions, your aspirations, and your dreams.

## Explore, Develop, and Reinvent Yourself

In Howard Gardner's book *Leading Minds* he states,

*"More so than in the case of other leaders, [Eleanor] Roosevelt and [Martin Luther] King found themselves reinventing themselves from time to time — partly in response to the stirring events of their own lives, partly in response to reactions from the most responsive members of their audiences."*

The success you will discover in your life in part will come from your ability to reinvent yourself both personally and professionally. The world is changing so rapidly that if you don't transform your image, thoughts, or career focus, you'll run the risk of missing opportunities as they come your way.

Dr. Rhonda Waters, Ph.D. of the Mutare Group is a classic example of personal reinvention. With nearly two decades of service in a Boston telephone company, Waters carefully planned her exit strategy before launching her career development company in 2000. She reinforced her financial nest egg, sharpened her Internet skills, and stepped out into the wild world of entrepreneurship. In the process, she returned to school and completed her doctorate. Dr. Waters now uses her telecommunications experience in the workshops and consulting projects she conducts on career development, career transitions, and project management.

If you're going to grow, you must change. If you're going to change, you must identify new opportunities to reinvent yourself. Empowerment requires change. As you expand your horizons, figure out new ways to reinvent yourself for future success.

# *Life*

is certainly not fair,

and it is not easy.

The best advice

I can give you is

don't quit, don't give up,

and keep moving!

# CHAPTER TEN

# Empowerment Begins When You Believe In Yourself

## Belief in Yourself

Every one of my Personal Empowerment Radio Tips ends with my special brand of turbocharged energy: Empowerment Begins When You Believe In Yourself.

The journey to self development begins and ends with you. The empowerment process is that journey that will sharpen your skills, enhance your understanding of the world around you and generate a personal developmental awareness level that will guide you in the future.

Life is certainly not fair, and it is not easy. You will experience difficulties, setbacks and obstacles that may cause you to question your ability to resolve your problems. The best advice I can give you is don't quit, don't give up, and keep moving! You have formulated your vision, and you know what you need to do to move ahead. As I stated in the previous chapter, keep stepping. Expect the naysayers to heckle you, but don't let them stop you. Keep your cool, call up your faith, and don't stop until you reach your goal.

## Friends Helping Friends

My first book project involved a chapter I wrote in a women's anthology titled *Sisters Together: Lessons Learned That Have Anchored Our Souls*. The book was the brainchild of my two friends and colleagues, Debra Washington Gould and Nancy Lewis. My chapter was a tribute to my son and gave the reader insight into how to have a conversation with someone who has lost a child. The book was a wonderful healing process for me, and allowed some relief from the pain and anguish I felt in those early days following his death.

In the book other women expressed the joys and sorrows of life, and shared the countless ways that their strength and empowerment helped them to move through the madness of life. Nancy Lewis wrote a chapter entitled, *"Drop The Baggage And Move Forward."* In it she shared the anxiety she felt when reconnecting with her father after many years of absence.

Forgiveness was her key, and she states, *"Remember, unforgiveness is unhealthy and forgiveness cleanses the soul."*

Who in your life can you forgive today? Is there a way that the baggage that's holding you back can be lifted so you can move on to more important duties? Can you let go of your anger, disappointment, and anguish by confronting your past sorrows and bidding them a permanent goodbye?

Are there ways that you face your fears by realizing the power you have to stop them dead in their tracks? Are you big enough to grow beyond your weaknesses?

Remember the accountability team I talked about in Chapter Two of this book? Debra Washington Gould describes her very own accountability team in her chapter of *Sisters Together*. Titled *"Friends Helping Friends,"* Debra describes a weekly business lunch meeting where each participant shared their dreams and aspirations with each other. In essence, they had actually formed an accountability team, each one helping the other to succeed. Debra's efforts in the group transformed her from being a government employee to a successful entrepreneur.

In the chapter she advised the reader to *"find yourself some trusted friends to open up to. In any endeavor, you need friends to listen, support and encourage you. Friends will not judge you and block your growth and maturity. It's your dream."*

It is your dream. It is your life. Seek out those trusted friends who will support your passion to succeed life. Surround yourself with the goodness of trusted friends.

## Call On Your Inner Strength

In our diverse world, inner strength can be defined many different ways. No matter what your faith, Christian, Muslim, Jewish, Buddhist, Hindu, or New Age thinker, a belief in a Higher power can see you through your difficulties. For me, prayer, my belief in God, and the loving support of my family and church helped me through the darkness that I've faced over the years.

Assess how you gather your inner strength, and then call on it when the tough times come. Remember that some challenges are much bigger than you are. Connecting with that Higher power will protect and shield you from the emotional roller coaster rides of life.

## Talk to Others

So often we keep all of our troubles bottled up inside. We tell ourselves, "Nobody else is going through what I am. People just don't understand my problems." Our self-talk can be quite powerful.

We forget that there may be a colleague, a trusted friend, a family member, or a business associate who has just experienced the exact same challenge that you now face. I found that out very quickly after my son died, when three other mothers lost their bright and gifted sons in tragic accidents within two weeks of my son's death. I realized that the human experience is shared by all of us. Life spares no one when it comes to facing difficult times. So swallow your pride and reach out to someone who can support you.

## Don't Lose Your Sense of Humor

Even in the depths of your despair humor can bring a welcome change of attitude. Believe it or not, one of the moments I remember vividly during that fateful week in June, 1997, centered on the funny stories my daughter, Lorna, shared at my son's funeral. Kids' stories. Stories that made me laugh. Stories that dried the tears running down my cheeks. Humorous reflections that we could all relate to.

For those of you who are battling cancer or who have loved ones who are fighting that dreaded disease, visit Christine Clifford's website **www.CancerClub.com.** Christine, a breast cancer survivor and professional speaker, has developed a wonderful approach to life, and shares her humorous touch with others via the Internet. For her company logo, she even uses the profile of an attractive woman sporting a bald head. Christine is an example that, in spite of your circumstances, humor can help buffer life's booby traps and pitfalls.

## Bounce Back

If you don't believe much else, do understand that today's challenges will become tomorrow's memories. They may be forgettable memories, but they'll be memories nonetheless. When you concentrate on facing your challenges and resolving your issues, tomorrow will come much more quickly.

The emotional impact from the loss of loved ones, divorce, extreme financial woes, catastrophic illnesses or job loss won't always go away in a flash.

What you must tell yourself is that you will overcome your circumstances and you cannot quit.

Speaking, writing, and consulting have been the healing instruments in my life. The opportunity of addressing audiences and sharing my personal stories with others has helped me to bounce back and reposition my life by adding more purpose, commitment, and dedication into the work that I do.

You, too, can bounce back from your troubles each time life's bottomless pit reaches up to grabs you. Take a deep breath, think on your feet, connect with others, find your inner strength, and remember that tomorrow's sunshine is right around the corner.

## Step Forward With Your Empowerment

It's all up to you! The world is waiting for your laughter, your joy, your mistakes, and your passion. No matter what it is, your visions will lead to bigger dreams and goals that you will embrace in your life. Focus on your vision and follow your dreams. And remember that empowerment begins when you believe in yourself.

*Find your purpose*
and you will find the path
that will make your life
an important part of
the human experience.
Step forward and empower
yourself to success.

# Resource Directory
## for Empowerment Success

### Chapter One:
### Defining Empowerment

*Going Deep in Life and Leadership* by Ian Percy
1997. Toronto, Ontario, Canada: Macmillan Canada.

*Celebrate The Temporary* by Clyde Reid
1972. New York. Harper & Row.

### Chapter Two:
### Creating Your Vision

*Illuminating The Spirit: A Guided Journal for Inviting Energy and Change Into Your Life*
by Audra Bohannon and Verna Ford
2003. Jersey City, New Jersey. Pushkin Management Group, LLC.

*Encyclopedia Of Home Designs.*
1998. Tucson, Arizona. Home Planners.

*The Journey Inward: A Guide To Prayer & Reflection*
 by Jessica Kendall Ingram
1996. Detroit, Michigan. Journey Press.

## Other Resources for Chapter Two

*"January Is Vision Month"*
Bethel AME Church
Rev. Drs. Ray and Gloria-White Hammond
215 Forest Street
Boston, MA 02130
(617) 524-7900
www.BethelAME.org

## Chapter Three:
# *Getting Through the Storms of Life*

*Angel Threads: Inspirational Stories of*
*How Angels Weave the Tapestry of Our Lives*
By Robert J. Danzigwith Callie Rucker-Oettinger
2000. Hollywood, Florida. Frederick Fell Publishers, Inc.

*What's Going On Lord?*
*Finding Calm in the Midst of the Storm*
by Thelma Wells
1999. Nashville. Thomas Nelson, Inc.

*Kujua: A Spirituality Of The Hidden Way*
by Cecilia Williams Bryant
1993. Baltimore, Maryland. Akosua Visions.

## Other Resources for Chapter Two

*Bi-Annual Mock Car Accident and Fatality*
Milton Public Schools • Milton, Massachusetts
(617) 698-4809

*Compassionate Friends*
The Compassionate Friends is a national nonprofit, self-help support organization that offers friendship and understanding to bereaved parents, grandparents and siblings.
www.CompassionateFriends.org

*June Is Student Safety Month*
www.TellCarole.com

*Music That Helped Carole Cope With Losing Her Son*
"Farther Along"
Sung By Bishop Carlton Pearson
CD: Live At Azusa 2
www.azusa.org
www.wbr.com/blackmusic/CARLTON

## Activist Organizations

Mothers Against Drunk Driving (MADD)
www.madd.org

Students Against Destructive Decisions
(Students Against Drunk Driving) SADD
www.saddonline.com

## Chapter Four:
## *Mental Toughness*

*10 Good Choices That Empower Black Women's Lives*
by Grace Cornish,
2000. New York. Crown Publishers.

*The Prophet* by Kahlil Gibran
2001. New York. Alfred A Knopf.

*Burn This Book and Move On With Your Life*
by Jessica Hurley
2002. Kansas City. Andrews McMeel Publishing.

*In The Spirit* by Susan L. Taylor
1993. New York. Amistad.

*Until Today! Daily Devotions for*
*Spiritual Growth and Peace of Mind*
by Iyanla Vanzant
2000. New York. Simon & Schuster.

*Women's Devotional Bible: New International Version (NIV)*
1991. Grand Rapids, Michigan. Zondervan Publishing House.


## Other Resources for Chapter Four

*Music that Helped Carole Cope with Tough Times*
"We Shall Not Be Moved"
Sung by Sweet Honey In The Rock
CD or Audio Tape: *Still The Same Me*
www.SweetHoney.com

## Chapter Five:
## *Empowerment Through Career Advancement*

*Wake 'Em Up: How To Use Humor and Other Professional Techniques To Create Alarmingly Good Business Presentations*
by Tom Antion
1999. Landover Hills, Maryland. Anchor Publishing.

*The Leader Of the Future*
by Richard Beckhard, Marshall Goldsmith, and Frances Hesselbein
The Drucker Foundation Future Series
1996. New York. Jossey-Bass.

*The Leader Within You:*
*Master 9 Powers To Be the Leader*
*You Always Wanted To Be*
by Robert J. Danzig with Howard Kaplan
1998. Hollywood, Florida. Lifetime Books, Inc.

*The Miracles Of Mentoring*
by Thomas W. Dortch, Jr., and
The 100 Black Men Of America, Inc
2000. New York. Doubleday.

*Indispensable Employees:*
*How To Hire Them How To Keep Them*
by Martha Fields, R.A.
2001. Franklin Lakes, NJ. Career Press.

*Care Packages For The Workplace:*
*Dozens of Little Things You Can Do*
*To Regenerate Spirit at Work*
by Barbara A.Glanz
1996. New York. McGraw-Hill.

*Disney Magic:*
*Business Strategy You Can Use*
*at Work and at Home*
by Rich Hamilton
2003. Phoenix, Arizona. Sell Better Tools.

*Dealing With People*
by Robert Heller
1999. New York. DK Publishing.

*Office Politics: Seizing Power, Wielding Clout*
by Marilyn Kennedy
1980. New York. Warner Books.

*Soul Proprietor:*
*101 Lessons from a Lifestyle Entrepreneur*
by Jane Pollak
2001. Freedom, California. The Crossing Press.

*The Personal Touch:*
*What You Really Need To Succeed*
*In Today's Fast-paced Business World*
by Terrie Williams
1994. New York. Warner Books.

*Only Wet Babies Like Change:*
*Workplace Wisdom for Baby Boomers*
Mary-FrancesWinters
2002. Springfield, Virginia. Renaissance Publishers, Inc.

## Other Resources for Chapter Five

*Business Management, Empowerment, and Leadership*
Carole Copeland Thomas
(508) 947-5755 • (800) 947-5755
www.TellCarole.com

*Executive Coach Training and Services*
Coach University
www.CoachInc.com

*International Coach Federation*
www.CoachFederation.org

*Mentoring*
Dr. Stacy Blake Beard • (617) 521-3833
Simmons College Center For Gender and Organization
Boston, Massachusetts

*Networking for African Americans*
FraserNet
George Fraser • (216) 691-6686
www.FraserNet.com

*Salary Comparison Across Industries*
www.Salary.com

## Chapter Six:
# *Diversity In A Global World*

### *Growing Up Latino: Memoirs and Stories*
by Harold Augenbraum and Ilan Stavans
1993. Boston/New York. Houghton Mifflin Company.

### *Before The Mayflower: A History of Black America*
by Lerone Bennett, Jr.
1988. New York. Penguin Books.

### *The Diversity Advantage:*
### *A Guide To Making Diversity Work*
Lenora Billings-Harris
1998. Greensboro, North Carolina, Oakhill Press.

### *Breaking The Barrier Of Bias*
by Tracy Brown
**www.DiversityTrends.com.**

### *Madame C.J.Walker: Entrepreneur*
by A'Lelia Perry Bundles
1991. New York/Philadelphia. Chelsea House Publishers.

### *Human Communications, Third Edition*
by Michael Burgoon, Edwin Dawson and Frank G. Hunsaker
1994. Thousand Oaks, California. SAGE Publications, Inc.

### *The Chinese In America*
by Iris Chang
2003. New York. Viking.

*Understanding Diversity: Readings, Cases and Exercises*
by Carol Harvey and M. June Allard
1995. New York. Harper Collins College Publishers.

*Workforce 2020: Work and Workers in the 21st Century*
by Richard Judy and Carol D'Amico
1999. Indianapolis, Indiana. Hudson Institute.

*Through Harsh Winters:*
*The Life of a Japanese Immigrant Woman*
by Akemi Kikumura
1981. Novato, California. Chandler & Sharp Publishers, Inc.

*Respect: An Exploration*
by Sara Lawrence-Lightfoot
2000. Cambridge, Massachusetts. Perseus Books.

*Lies My Teacher Told Me:*
*Everything Your American History Textbook Got Wrong*
by James W. Loewen
1995. New York. The New York Press.

*John Adams*
by David McCullough
2001. New York. Simon & Schuster.

*World Facts & Maps*
by Rand McNally
2000. Rand McNally.

*Out in the Workplace:*
*The Pleasures and Perils of Coming Out on the Job*
by Richard Rasi and Lourdes Rodriguez-Nogues
1995. Los Angeles, California. Alyson Publications.

*Breaking Through: The Making of*
*Minority Executives in Corporate America*
by David Thomas and John Gabarro
1999. Boston. Harvard Business School Press.

*Redefining Diversity*
by R. Roosevelt Thomas, Jr.
1996. New York. Amacom.

## Other Resources for Chapter Six

*Affirmative Action Policies*

United States Department Of Labor
**www.dol.gov**

Office of Federal Contract Compliance Programs
**www.dol.gov/esa/ofccp**

*Demographic, Ethnic and Population Data*
Culture Grams
Perspective on daily life, culture, history, customs,
and society of the world's people
**www.CultureGrams.com**

United States Census Bureau
www.census.gov

The World Factbook
www.cia.gov/cia/publications/factbook

## Diversity Consultant
Carole Copeland Thomas
(508) 947-5755 • (800) 801-6599
www.TellCarole.com

## Diversity Magazine
Diversity, Inc
www.DiversityInc.com

## Diversity Online Publication
www.UnityFirst.com

## Diversity Website
www.DiversityInc.com

## Languages of the World
SIL International (Summer Institute of Linguistics)
www.sil.org
www.ethnologue.com

## Religions of the World
www.ReligiousTolerance.org

# Chapter Seven:
## *Family Matters*

*My Mother Myself:*
*The Daughter's Search for Identity*
by Nancy. Friday
1997. New York. Delta.

*Your Family Reunion:*
*How To Plan It, Organize It, and Enjoy It*
by George Morgan
2001. Provo, Utah. Ancestry Publishing.

*The Everything Online Genealogy Book:*
*Use the Web to Discover Long Lost Relations,*
*Trace Your Family Tree Back to Royalty*
*and Share Your History with Far-Flung Cousins*
by Pat Richley
2001. Avon, Massachusetts. Adams Media.

*Tea Celebrations*
by Alexandra Stoddard
1994. New York. Avon Books.

*The Charms of Tea*
by Victoria Magazine
1991. New York. Hearst Books.

*Finding a Place Called Home: A Guide to*
*African-American Genealogy and Historical Identity*
by Dee Palmer Woodtor
1999. New York. Random House.

## Other Resources for Chapter Seven

### Documentary
Standing in the Shadows of Motown
Format: DVD or VHS • Audio Soundtrack: CD
www.artisanent.com

### Family Reunion Conference for All Ethnic Groups
Family Reunion Conference presented by
The Family Reunion Institute of
Temple University and
Pathfinders Travel Magazine
www.temple.edu/fri/familyreunion
www.PathfindersTravel.com

### Genealogy Research
www.Ancestry.com

www.RootsWeb.com

www.Genealogy.com

www.MyFamily.com

www.Ancestry.co.uk

### Northeast Document Conservation Center
Andover, Massachusetts
(978) 475-6021
www.nedcc.org

### Supplies and Resources for Preserving Collectables
Archival Catalog and Gaylord Catalog
(800) 448-6160
www.Gaylord.com

## Chapter Eight:
## *Self Care*

*Communicate With Confidence:*
*How To Say It Right the First Time and Every Time*
by Dianna Booher
1994 New York. McGraw-Hill, Inc.

*The Art of Living Single*
by Michael Broder
1988. New York. Avon Books.

*Prime Time: The African American Woman's*
*Complete Guide to Midlife Health and Wellness*
by Marilyn Hughes Gaston, MD and Gayle K. Porter
2001. New York. One World Ballantine Books.

*Mayo Clinic Family Health Book, Third Edition*
by the Mayo Clinic
2003. New York. HarperResource.

*Sassy, Single & Satisfied:*
*Secrets to Loving the Life You're Living*
by Michelle McKinney Hammond
2003. Eugene, Oregon. Harvest House Publisher.

*Secrets of an Irrestistible Woman:*
*Smart Rules for Capturing His Heart*
by Michelle McKinney Hammond
1998. Eugene, Oregon. Harvest House Publisher.

*Dining with the Duchess*
by Sarah, the Duchess of York and Weight Watchers
1998. New York. Simon & Schuster.

*List Yourself: Listmaking as the Way to Self-Discovery*
Ilene Segalove and Paul Bob Velick
1996. Kansas City. Andrews and McMeel.

*Legacy: A Step-by-Step Guide*
*to Writing Personal History*
by Linda Spence
1997. Athens. Swallow Press/Ohio University Press.

## Other Resources for Chapter Eight

*Managing Stress for Women*
Calm Spirit: A Woman's Guide to Managing Stress (CD)
by Thulani DeMarsay
The Center For Personal Development
(617) 436-8689
www.MyCalmSpirit.com

*Spa Resorts*
**Doral Golf Resort & Spa**
Miami, Florida
www.DoralResort.com

*Weight Watchers*
www.WeightWatchers.com

## Chapter Nine:
### *Take Action*

*Leading Minds: An Anatomy of Leadership*
by Howard Gardner with Emma Laskin
1995. New York. Basic Books.

*Let Me See Your Body Talk*
by Jan Hargrave
1995. Dubuque, Iowa. Kendall/Hunt Publishing Company.

*Get Along, Get Ahead:*
*101 Courtesies for the New Workplace*
by Karen Hinds
2000. Boston. New Books Publishing.

*What Makes the Great Great:*
*Strategies for Extraordinary Achievement*
by Dennis P. Kimbro
1998. New York. Doubleday.

*101 Ways To Promote Yourself*
by Raleigh Pinskey
1997. New York. Avon.

*Wealth Happens One Day at a Time:*
*365 Days to a Brighter Financial Future*
by Brooke Stephens
1999. New York. HarperBusiness.

*Career Transitions: A Proactive Approach Workbook*
by Rhonda F. Waters, PhD
2001. Boston. Mutare Group
**www.MutareGroup.com.**

## Other Resources for Chapter Nine

*Financial Consulting*
Investor's Workshops of America
Ray Barrows
(508) 984-3331

*Memory Project*
National Scrapbook Day by Creative Memories
Robin Thompson
**www.RobinThompson.com**

## Chapter Ten:
# *Empowerment Begins When You Believe In Yourself*

*Sisters Together:*
*Lessons Learned that have Anchored our Souls*
by Debra Washington Gould and Nancy Lewis
1998. Fayetteville, Georgia. Manson & Gould Publishing.

*Take the Bully by the Horns:*
*Stop Unethical, Uncooperative,*
*or Unpleasant People from*
*Running and Ruining Your Life*
by Sam Horn
2002. New York. St Martin's Press.


## Website Resources

*Cancer Support Resource*
Christine Clifford
**www.CancerClub.com**

# *About the Author*

**Carole Copeland Thomas** is the voice of personal empowerment. She is a keynote speaker, empowerment expert, diversity professional and leadership consultant in C. Thomas & Associates, a business she started in 1987. Ms. Thomas served as an adjunct faculty member for Bentley College for a decade, and has spoken throughout the United States, London, England, Canada, and Australia.

## Carole the Author

Carole is also the publisher of the weekly electronic newsletter, **Empowerment Today**, distributed to subscribers throughout the world. She has also published several articles, business cases, and essays in trade magazines and academic textbooks

## The Media Calls on Carole

Carole has been featured on ABC Radio, CBS-TV, and Fox News-TV. She has also been featured in Black Enterprise Magazine, the Boston Globe and the Boston Herald. Carole is a contributor to the USA Today Small Business Panel.

## Syndicated Radio Host

For three years Carole's Personal Empowerment Tips were heard daily on Boston's WILD 1090 AM Radio. Her one hour call-in radio talk show, "Focus On Empowerment" was heard every Friday morning on the station. Carole's syndicated radio tips were broadcast in 10 US cities and were sponsored by Marshalls, the nationwide off-price retail store.

## Education

A native of Detroit, Michigan, Carole is an experienced entrepreneur with awards and achievements in sales, marketing, and management. After graduating with honors in 1975 from Emory University in Atlanta, Carole developed a sales management career with Mary Kay Cosmetics, winning a pink car in 1980. She returned to graduate school in 1983 (on a Martin Luther King, Jr. academic fellowship), and received her MBA degree from Northeastern University in Boston. Continuing on a career path in bank marketing and later The Gillette Company, Carole transitioned into the human service industry and served as the branch sales manager for a national temporary employment agency. She started her own firm in 1987.

## Carole the Mother

Carole is the mother of three children:

**Lorna,** a University of Hartford doctoral student

**Michelle,** a Chicago State University undergraduate student,

and the late **Mickarl D. Thomas, Jr.**

## Carole's Personal Motto:

*Empowerment Begins When You Believe In Yourself.*

# *Professional Speaking Services*

For your next convention, conference, meeting, workshop, retreat, or staff session you can count on the speaking services of Carole Copeland Thomas.

Specializing in empowerment, diversity, leadership, youth issues and women, Carole's message will leave a lasting impression with your audience.

To Book Carole, Contact her at:
400 W. Cummings Park  Suite 1725-154
Woburn, Massachusetts  01801

## (508) 947-5755 - Office

## (800) 801-6599 - Toll Free

(508) 947-3903 - Fax • Carole@TellCarole.com - email

Sign up for Carole's Online Newsletter at:

## www.TellCarole.com

**Speaking • Training • Consulting • Facilitation**

# PERSONAL EMPOWERMENT

## How To Turbocharge Your Life
## Both On and Off Your Job
## — Order Form —

Name (Please Print)

Organization

Shipping Address                                     Suite/Apt#

City                            State                        Zip

Daytime Phone                        Home Phone

Email Address

## Payment Method

___ Money Order    ___ Check    ___ American Express    ___ Visa    ___ Master Card

Send _____ books at $ 15.00 each          _____

Shipping & handling                  _____          Shipping & Handling
                                                          $4.00 for the 1st book
+ 5% Sales Tax (MA residents only)   _____             $2.00 for each
                                                            additional book
                    TOTAL PAYMENT:   _____

Credit Card Number                                   Expiration Date

Cardholder Name                          Signature

**www.TellCarole.com** • Email: Carole@TellCarole.com
Tel: 1-800-801-6599 or (508) 947-5755 • Fax: (508) 947-3903

### Please clip and mail to: C. Thomas & Associates
**400 W. Cummings Park Suite 1725-154, Woburn, MA 01801**

Please make your check payable to C. Thomas & Associates

For bulk orders and special discount pricing call Carole at **(508) 947-5755**

# More Praise for
# PERSONAL EMPOWERMENT

Carole's book has the warmth and charm of sitting on a porch swing, sharing stories about life and lessons learned. She captures both the painful memories and the joyful times, showing us how we can learn from her experiences.

*– Robin Thompson*
*Thompson Training &*
*Keynote Presentations, Inc.*

Carole has dedicated her talents and worklife to empowering individuals to be all that they can be, to contribute to society, and to be fulfilled.

*– Frank X. McCarthy, President*
*Diverse Workforce, Inc.*

Carole makes personal empowerment real and attainable by providing more than just motivation. It's a formula for discovering, developing, and enjoying a powerful way of living.

*– Karen Hinds, Author, President*
*Karen Hinds Seminars*

Carole practices what she preaches. Her book offers a wealth of knowledge on empowering an individual both personally and professionally.

*– Debra Washington Gould*
*Co-author of Sisters Together: Lessons*
*Learned That Have Anchored Our Souls*

Stop hesitating and waiting for your life to improve—take charge and buy this book! Carole Copeland Thomas tells us how to get going and stay in motion through engaging stories and action plans.

*– Dr. Rhonda F. Waters, Ph.D.*
*President and CEO*
*The Mutare Group, Inc.*